THE Freedom OF A Christian

THE
Freedom
OF A
Christian

Luther's Significance for Contemporary Theology

EBERHARD JÜNGEL

*Translated by
Roy A. Harrisville*

AUGSBURG Publishing House • Minneapolis

THE FREEDOM OF A CHRISTIAN
Luther's Significance for Contemporary Theology

Scripture quotations, unless otherwise noted, are from the Revised Standard Version of the Bible, copyright 1946, 1952, and 1971 by the Division of Christian Education of the National Council of Churches.

Library of Congress Cataloging-in-Publication Data

Jüngel, Eberhard.
    [Zur Freiheit eines Christenmenschen. English]
    The freedom of a Christian : Luther's significance for
contemporary theology / Eberhard Jüngel ; translated by Roy A.
Harrisville.
      p.   cm.
    Translation of: Zur Freiheit eines Christenmenschen.
    Bibliography: p.
    ISBN 0-8066-2393-4
    1. Freedom (Theology) 2. Luther, Martin, 1483-1546. Von der
Freiheit eines christenmenschen. I. Title.
BT810.2.J8313 1988
233'.7—dc19
                                     88-22304
                                         CIP

Manufactured in the U.S.A.   APH 10-2380

1 2 3 4 5 6 7 8 9 0 1 2 3 4 5 6 7 8 9

Contents

Abbreviations

BHTh	Beiträge zur historischen Theologie
CChr. SL	Corpus Christianorum. Serie Latina
CSEL	Corpus scriptorum ecclesiasticorum Latinorum
HWP	*Historisches Wörterbuch der Philosophie*
LCL	Loeb Classical Library
LW	*Luther's Works* (American Edition)
WA	Weimar Ausgabe
WA.B	Weimar Ausgabe, *Briefe*
WA.TR	Weimar Ausgabe, *Tischreden*
ZThK	*Zeitschrift für Theologie und Kirche*

Translator's Preface

It is rumored about Tübingen that Eberhard Jüngel boasts his books cannot be translated into English. The appearance in English of his volume, *God as the Mystery of the World,* translated by Darrel Guder, is evidence that they can in fact be translated. But it is also a fact that they cannot be translated with ease. Jüngel's works yield prime illustration of the foreigner's frustration with that "horrible German language," celebrated by Mark Twain, and more recently in such volumes as Gordon Craig's *The Germans.* Jüngel pelts his readers with adverbs, double negatives, and neologisms. He heaps up subordinate clauses which send the translator scurrying to and fro in search of their relatives and antecedents—all of which renders the work of translating less an enjoyment than sheer labor (and, perhaps, with little thanks from the author!).

Still, for all his "arrogant" style, Jüngel deserves translation. He does so because his is one of the few clear voices within contemporary theological discussion, a discussion which speaks to "everything and everyone" (his own words), but which is without any orientation or object of its own. Others may be able to speak clearly, but what makes Jüngel deserve to be heard is that his grasp of classical theological tradition, the tradition of the 16th century and the current theological situation, together with the challenges hurled at it in contemporary thought, sets him apart from the majority, here and in Europe. The great "soloists" in theology may be dead and gone, but there are still some powerful voices left in the choir. Jüngel's is one of them.

This little book, whose essential contents were delivered at the Lund Congress of Luther researchers, and for reasons of length threw its hearers into pandemonium, deserves translation. It is devoted to the question of Luther's significance for theology today, and by way of an exposition of his treatise on *The Freedom of a Christian.* For years, that gem has gone begging for a proper setting, to say nothing of a setting or exposition with significance for the here and now. This book also deserves translation because it encompasses themes treated at length in Jüngel's earlier translated work, thus serving as its introduction.

Despite the care given to translate Jüngel into intelligible English, whatever struggle the reader may still face in the reading of this text will be well worth the trouble—and for the sake of its content. As the author himself suggests, the "lay reader" is encouraged to begin with the book's third chapter, first, because it contains the heart of the argument, and second, because (happily) it is easier to grasp. Thus is affectation abandoned when an author means to be understood!

One little word comprises the principal difficulty in translating this volume—the word *Mensch*. As any schoolboy or schoolgirl knows, every German noun has its gender. Accordingly, the masculine article has been assigned to *Mensch*. But the word does not denote the male. "Person" or "human being," even "humanity" may serve as surrogate—until we encounter sentences in which adjectives such as "inner" or "outer" are affixed to it, and both of them predicated of a third *Mensch!* In a few instances, it was possible to circumvent use of the phrase "inner man" or "outer man." In most, it was not, without doing violence to Luther's distinctions, to Jüngel's exposition of those distinctions, and thus to intelligibility. Finally, the terms "self" and "nature" were unable to bear the load.

Where translations exist, references in the footnotes to Luther's works are cited according to the Weimar Edition, followed by their counterparts in the American Edition *(Luther's Works),* prepared by Jaroslav Pelikan and associates. References to *The Freedom of a Christian* are given according to the bilingual text of L. E. Schmitt, also followed by their translation in the American Edition. It will be obvious to the reader, or indicated in the notes, where no translation exists.

ROY A. HARRISVILLE

12

Foreword

Above the portal of Tübingen University, now celebrating its 500th Jubilee, appears a word which as its founder's motto also claims to express the academic self-understanding of those who teach and learn: *Attempto.* I attempt, I venture.

When I received the request to deliver the main lecture on "Luther's Significance for Contemporary Theology" at the Fifth International Congress of Luther Research at Lund, I had a particular reason for recalling the motto of my Tübingen alma mater. The difficulties of such an undertaking were clear; the limits of my competence were obvious. Yet, paradoxically, I felt encouraged by the difficulty of the task assigned me, since it is suited to reduce to insignificance once more the distance between those who are somewhat (or even very much) at home in the many and weighty volumes of the Weimar Edition of Luther's works, and those who are somewhat (or even a great deal) less at home in them. In addition, it stimulated me to give account of the degree the Reformer's theology influenced me in the elaboration of ideas set forth in my book *God as the Mystery of the World.*[1]

It also happened that, after a few sessions in the winter semester of 1976–1977, I had discontinued a seminar on Luther's treatise *The Freedom of a Christian.* This educational institution had been profoundly disturbed during a so-called strike. Continuance of the seminar had become impossible, even for acoustical reasons. In retrospect I regard this measure as appropriate. The abrupt end to the seminar, which till then had proceeded in an especially gratifying and fruitful way, troubled me no less than the students angry over the disruption—which was indeed, from their point of view, justifiable. In this situation I gladly seized the opportunity which the Luther scholars gave me—by means of a theological reminiscence of Luther's treatise on freedom—to deliver in writing what I had intended to contribute orally to that seminar. I suppose the written composition would have had a different aspect if the dialogs and debates with students could have been continued. Yet, quite a number of the questions with which a student study group emerging out of that interrupted seminar pursued me at the end of the semester have found their way into this little monograph. It attempts to uncover Luther's significance for contemporary theology—remarkable choice of theme!—by way of a few of his basic theological distinctions, above all, his understanding of Christian freedom. Its goal will be achieved when students and pastors, perhaps also a few other Christians, will not shun the bit of exertion and reflection needed to handle Luther's classical tractate and to steep themselves in it.

The monograph is divided thusly: First, the usual difficulty attaching to our capacity for supplying information about the contemporary significance of past events is at least briefly considered. Various formulations of the question are considered within which Luther's significance for contemporary theology could be discussed (chap. 1). Next, one of these possibilities, if not realized, should still be tested in an attempt to recite to what extent Luther has become significant, or more precisely, helpful to me in the perception of my own theological responsibilities (chaps. 2–3). I will not discuss to what degree Luther seems to me to burden contemporary theology, though this is a no less interesting and even somewhat important question.

The paraphrase of Luther's treatise in chapter 3 is prefaced in chapter 2 by a longer exercise in a few signal events of theological reflection, and to which Reformation theology has given impetus. But it may be useful, particularly for the "nontheologian," to begin by reading chapter 3, which in some respects is more easily understood. Looking back on the Lund Congress, I note with pleasure that the discussions during this Fifth International Congress of Luther Research—and, even more, the discussions which did not take place there—have thoroughly convinced me of the need for that task which the Luther researchers had set me and themselves, that is, to inquire into Luther's significance for contemporary theology.

1

•

The Question of Luther's Significance for Contemporary Theology

Formulation of the Question

1

Whoever would speak of Luther's significance for contemporary theology can do so in various ways.

One can attempt to investigate Luther's significance in terms of his *historical effects*. One can thus inquire into the *future* of that remote historical phenomenon, a future it possesses because of its "magnitude," as it once was called. The present, and contemporary theology with it, would then be of interest as one among many phases of Luther's effects.

Our own time belongs to the history of Luther's effects, entirely apart from whether it is conscious of how much it owes that other, remote, temporal event. The significance of important past events is always greater than appears significant about them at any given present, historical moment. In fact, the sum total of all the significances ever perceived of such an event is always less than a significant event *actually* portends. Truly significant events *have their effects,* entirely apart from whether they are perceived as such at any present moment. For this reason we must distinguish the *verification* of the significance of past events from their *actual significance.* Luther's theology as well, even Luther as historical event—inconceivable apart from his theology—is such an event. Its effect is never absorbed in its significance for this or that present moment. As a result, we will do well not to confuse Luther's possible significance for contemporary theology with his actual significance. Due to his historical potency, only one aspect of the significance of that remote event called "Luther" can be dealt with. The historical potency of a past history is never identical with its effects, not even with their sum—and certainly not with what we are able to perceive as effective or significant for us. The historical potency of a past reality is not identical with any reality sprung from it. It is rather the *capacity for having an effect,* any effect, or—often indirectly—for having such a continually new effect that it has a future.

Naturally, research which inquires into Luther's significance on these terms faces the problem of being utterly unable to foresee how much of the future belongs to this historical phenomenon. It was for good reason that the historian Reinhard Wittram inquired, "Who can dare to depict Luther and the Reformation as though one knew their entire future? Might the 450 years since be only a few phases of their effect?"[1] But without knowing everything of their future, it is difficult to decide their actual significance for the present.

Another, easily understandable way of discussing the theme assigned may be to inquire of contemporary theology to what extent and in what sense it is related to Luther—whether in agreement, criticism, rejection, or otherwise, and by this means assign him significance. Then it would be appropriate to speak first of contemporary theology's mistrust of the theology of the Reformer, who stated that theology's true object is the "guilty and condemned person and the justifying or redeeming God," and expressly added that "whatever is sought outside that area of inquiry or object is totally in error and idle in theology, since in Holy Scripture we expect nothing regarding matters of property, health of the body, or welfare of the state, things given us all to manage, and all of which are created. . . . Thus theology is not related to this life, but belongs to another life than Adam possesses."[2] Of course, the defensive reactions on the part of contemporary theology against such penetratingly unequivocal statements suggest that we speak rather of Luther's lack of significance—in its own way actually significant—for contemporary theology.

We could certainly also speak of the significance which Luther could have for contemporary theology. For that purpose, of course, we would need a sufficiently solid historical understanding of Luther. But when do we have such an understanding of merely those life expressions in fixed written form which have found entry into the Weimar Edition? Do we have it when we can oppose to the one opinion, to the *videtur quod* (it appears that) and the evidence in favor of it, an opposite opinion, a *sed contra* (but on the other hand), with no less evidence from Luther's writings? How easily one's sight of the argument in a text is lost with this running to and fro, and the wood becomes a thicket! And for pure erudition no binding statement, no *respondeo dicendum* (I respond to say) is arrived at.

In such a situation we must make a choice. We may be enjoined to modesty by the insight that with even the greatest historical erudition we cannot give voice to more than a segment of the true significance of past historical phenomena. Then for one who dabbles in history such modesty which desists from interrupting the scholarly alternation of *videtur quod* and *sed contra*—would be altogether proper.

However, "only rascals are modest" (Goethe). And where theology is involved, I would rather be taken for immodest than for a rascal. To inquire into Luther's significance for contemporary theology no doubt means to inquire *theologically*. And, in any event, to inquire theologically means to inquire into the truth of faith. In this respect I have learned from Martin Luther that whoever has understood just one thing has understood everything.[3] Without being lured by this to false conclusions, I venture to recall Luther's opinion with reference to his own work: "The number of books on theology must be reduced and only the best ones published. It is not many books that make men learned, nor even reading. But it is a good book frequently read, no matter how small it is, that makes a man learned in the Scriptures and godly."[4] One cannot read often enough Luther's treatise on *The Freedom of a Christian*. The expositions which follow are designed to assist in the reading. They are reading helps which aim to make clear the actuality of that text, in order thus to furnish an idea of the significance which Luther could have for contemporary theology.

2

"History tells stories."[5] This hermeneutical principle applies unconditionally, even concerning the significance of past theological decisions for contemporary theology. So then, I venture to *narrate*. By studying a few of Luther's texts, I would like to tell what has become significant for me in face of our present theological situation. This will offer nothing new, but perhaps what has long been familiar in a not quite so familiar way, and thus a few ideas suggested by Luther.

First, I should really tell of my teachers whose variety in their relation to Luther—up to the marked suspicion the aging Karl Barth held him under—has certainly had more influence on my own attempts to become acquainted with Luther than I am conscious of. The experts, of course, will in any event confirm that. In this way, then—begging my teachers' pardon—I intend to tell of Luther's significance for contemporary theology—and, without hesitation, on my own responsibility.

3

It is obvious that with such an attempt our contemporary theological tasks, especially the perplexities which have overtaken contemporary theology, work on our sensibilities. Naturally, I do not ignore the danger that in understanding *past* reality—and in any case that means a reality which in part at least is unknown—we allow ourselves to be led by formulations of the question from our own point in time.[6] Still, it is true even of *contemporary* events that they are only inadequately disclosed to present consciousness: "The real sense for the histories of human beings is

only a late development, more under the quiet influences of recollection than under the more forceful impressions of the present."[7] How much more must this be said of the more forceful
impressions of a present moment which is not *simultaneous* with
past reality! But when we venture to study Luther's theology from
our current formulations of the question—more than that, when
we venture to test those formulations on the basis of his theology—then a compromise might be possible between "the more
forceful impressions of the present" and "the quiet influences of
recollection," a compromise that in any event is something less
than slothful.

"We Are to Be Human and Not God. This Is the Summa"

1

If contemporary theology has any central theme at all, it is Christian freedom. All current theological trends of importance claim
to battle for the *libertas christiana*. But this also means that this
central theme exists only as a matter in dispute. Indeed, the differences and contrasts between the various possible currents of
contemporary theology are explained not least by the fact that
they differ in the understanding of Christian freedom.

In addition, together with the *understanding* of Christian freedom, its *reality* is also at stake. The Christian *doctrine* of freedom,
even as an "academic concern,"[8] is a life force. It intends to
become actual, and—quite in contrast to Hegel's philosophy, for
example, which claims to paint its gray in gray only when a world
has grown old—understands itself as eagerly waiting for day to
break. Its urgent question reads: "Watcher, is the night nearly
past?" (Isa. 21:11). In contrast to the owl of Minerva, which
takes flight only when twilight sets in, it prays for the coming of
that liberating Spirit whose dove is revered as a harbinger of the
new day. The Christian doctrine of freedom presses toward a life
in freedom. Every thought longs for precisely that reality which
corresponds to it. Nowhere is Christian truth more intoxicated
with reality than in the struggle for freedom.

Intoxication with reality, however, hides a tendency to regulate the human being's relation to truth, so that the link to reality tends to divorce itself from obligation to the truth. It is evident that this danger threatens contemporary theology to a particular degree. In this situation such a topic as Luther's significance for contemporary theology can best be treated (without prejudice to the fact that we are all somehow, often indirectly, his heirs, and that in temporal and spiritual matters even our own time is constantly met by the distant effects of that historical phenomenon we call Luther) by drawing him into our own struggle for Christian freedom, under the assumption that he has something to say. That he has something to say will best be indicated by the *questions* with which he unsettles us. In order to raise such questions, we shall call to mind Luther's treatise on *The Freedom of a Christian*, justly described as "the most perfect expression" of Luther's "Reformation understanding of the mystery of Christ."[9]

But if the understanding of the mystery of Christ is involved in the Reformation understanding of Christian freedom, then this raises the question as to whether our struggle for freedom can deal at all with the question of the mystery of the person of Jesus Christ. Is the mystery of the person of Jesus Christ itself in dispute when the Christian's freedom is in dispute? Can we act as though the confession of Jesus Christ unites us, while it may be the proper understanding of Christian freedom in midst of this unity and confessional fellowship which divides, burdens, and can even separate us?

For Christian theology, the question as to who truly deserves to be called free cannot in fact be separated from the question concerning the person of Jesus Christ. In 1 Cor. 9:1, Paul linked the two questions—whether or not he was free and whether or not he was an apostle—to two further questions, whose clearly affirmative reply allows us to answer the first two with a yes. "Have I not seen Jesus our Lord? Are you not my workmanship in the Lord?" At the very beginning of his treatise, Luther quotes the statement shaped by Paul in that same chapter (1 Cor. 9:19): "For though I am free from all men, I have made myself a slave to all." [10] Without proof of the apostle's freedom in fellowship with Jesus Christ ("Have I not seen Jesus our Lord?") and without the apostolic activity deriving from this fellowship ("Are you not my workmanship in the Lord?") the sentence is meaningless. Thus, the freedom and service of the apostle whom Luther cites as the model of a Christian refer back to the mystery of the person of Jesus Christ and its effect. Luther at once expresses this (first in a quite superficial way) by pointing up the analogy between Christian existence and the being of Jesus Christ, in connection with Gal. 4:4 and Phil. 2:5ff.: "Although he was Lord of all, [he] was 'born of woman, born under the law,' and therefore was at the same time a free man and a servant, 'in the form of God' and 'of a servant.' " [11] To be sure, we must construe this analogy very strictly. Christian existence is in an analogous relation to the being of Jesus Christ only as *analogatum* (acted upon) and not as *analogans* (acting) in that relation (the being of Jesus Christ is therefore not to be construed merely as something to be imitated, but as working sacramentally). Luther implied this in the very first sentence of the German version of his treatise, when he more precisely defined the freedom of the Christian as "the freedom which Christ has won for him and given." [12] For Luther, a truer understanding of the analogy so structured requires a *fundamental, anthropological distinction,* which in light of the struggle for freedom raises further questions. Only within the horizon of this needed basic distinction can we explain to what extent the dispute over what deserves to be called freedom is a dispute over the person of Jesus Christ. And only the interpretation of the significance of Jesus Christ by way of this needed distinction makes clear to what extent everything is at stake in this dispute. But before we examine more carefully—within the context of Luther's treatise—this distinction which confirms the mystery of the person of Jesus Christ, we should recall not only the fact that but also the extent to which the theological art of properly distinguishing determines Luther's thought and speech throughout. Not least through this—seemingly purely formal—characteristic,

Luther's theology has had its effect and, if at all, can also have an effect today.

2

No doubt, one of the most striking characteristics of contemporary theology is its lack of orientation. This is indicated in the capriciousness of its themes. Contemporary theology speaks to everything and everyone. But by doing so, it has less and less specifically theological to say. It has no *thema probandum* (theme needing testing) of its own. If it had such a theme, then on the basis of it *everything* could in fact be theologically relevant. If the sentence of Thomas Aquinas is true, that "all things are dealt with in holy teaching in terms of God,"[13] then the converse must also be true, that everything can become the theme of theology on the basis of its relation to God. Since theology, on the basis of the object most peculiar to it, since theology as *speaking about God* necessarily aims at the whole, for this reason and to this extent it in fact has to do with "everything and everyone." But only for this reason and to this extent![14]

Speaking about God, however, aims *at the whole* only when it is *specific* to the greatest possible degree. Whoever says "God" speaks of a quite *specific,* unchangeable Being, whose particularity and unchangeability must also be of *greatest universal significance.* Accordingly, speaking about God must become *concrete* in the most specific way. But it must also be able to raise a *universal* claim in the most comprehensive way. How is this possible? How is it possible to speak of God in such a way that in, with, and under all the masks beneath which he hides, God himself concerns everyone unconditionally?

Whoever would speak of Luther in attempting to answer this question is tempted to offer a formula and to conjure up the distinction between law and gospel. I regard this as a correct response. Yet, I do not intend to *rehearse* it, but rather to tell of my attempts at approaching the learning of this high art. And here I must first recall a more formal trait of Luther's language which fascinated me while I was a student. I have in mind that peculiar inventiveness with which Luther can discuss both fairly complicated theological matters as well as the simplest events of elementary existence. The strictest scientific formulation, the tenderest expression, bitter irony, crude insult—these and many other habits of speech are united in a peculiar harmony, because they are all inventive, each in its own way. We may be as repulsed by certain dimensions of Luther's language as we are drawn irresistibly by others—the chorales! Even in his most offensive utterances he speaks in imaginative fashion.

In my opinion, this inventiveness in expression coincides with a basic rule of Luther's thought, and which he continually urges upon others, that is, that we must draw proper distinctions. Now, this is a common rule in debate, and thus as a purely formal directive is not particularly original. In fact, the bit of mental hygiene effected by this rule can definitely be carried too far, and as a distinction without letup can degenerate into sterility. In contrast, what gives Luther's instruction for drawing proper distinctions its peculiar power, a power explicit even in his language, is the orientation to those basic differences in which our life takes its course and with which theology is concerned. But since the basic differences in which human life is lived are as a rule obscured and hidden by the life process itself, it is precisely for the sake of life that *distinctions* must be made—between person and work, faith and love, law and gospel; between Christian person and person in the world, between doctrine and life, and so on. And it is at this point that Luther's theology, even in its language, has become particularly effective and helpful for me. It led me to make those basic distinctions—and, of course, to make others quite different from those learned from Luther!—which give to speaking about God a profile which makes it so sharp and interesting. Perhaps our contemporary theology is plagued by so many false alternatives not least because it must relearn the art of properly distinguishing from the ground up.

3

Most of the basic distinctions which have to do with theology and which especially give it profile as a speaking about God can of course be perceived even apart from theology. Who would not know how to distinguish between oneself and what one does, between flesh and spirit, outer and inner man, freedom and service, and so on? Yet the same basic distinctions assume a new status calculated to alter them when they encounter the proper, characteristic difference with which Christian theology is concerned. That difference is the distinction between God and humanity. Indeed, even apart from revelation and the theology which aims at its understanding, it is *supposed* that God and humanity are of two kinds. Naturally, we think that we at least know ourselves, and to that extent at least know what God is not, and can thus distinguish God and humanity. But according to Luther's understanding this is precisely humanity's self-deception. As early as in the *Disputation against Scholastic Theology* (1517), his point cannot be misunderstood: "Man is by nature unable to want God to be God. Indeed, he himself wants to be God, and does not want God to be God."[15] Thus, as Luther remarks a few years later in his exposition of Ps. 5:3, humans exist as unhappy and proud gods, who are first made truly human through the humanity of Jesus Christ: "Through the kingdom of his humanity, or (as the apostle says) through the kingdom of his flesh, occurring in faith, he conforms us to himself and crucifies us, by making out of unhappy and arrogant gods true men, i.e., miserable ones and sinners."[16] This assumes the *existence* of something like God. But human beings totally miss the *nature* of the God they assume to exist because they themselves want to be as God. They desire those very predicates of deity which apart from God's loving self-emptying as easily create a devil as a god. And human *reason* can no more maintain the Godhead of God than can the human *will*. Rather, as in the oft-cited passage from Luther's exposition of Jonah,[17] reason plays "blindman's buff" and "consistently gropes in the dark and misses the mark. It calls that God which is not God and fails to call Him God who really is God." The chief thing in Christian theology is that an end is put to this self-deception, and thus the proper distinction between God and humanity is reached. This is the fundamental distinction of Christian

24

theology. For in the last analysis, the revelation of God which it is the concern of Christian theology to understand means just this: for the good of humanity God himself intends the proper distinction between himself and humanity, a distinction which humanity by itself always neglects. In the above-cited exposition of Ps. 5:3, Luther stated that the very reason for God's becoming man in Jesus Christ is that humans become human. "For as in Adam we have risen to the image of God, so he has descended to our image, that he might lead us back to a knowledge of ourselves. And this takes place in the sacrament of his incarnation. This is the kingdom of faith, in which the cross of Christ reigns, which hurls pretended divinity down and summons perversely deserted humanity and the despised infirmity of the flesh to honor again." [18] God became man so that humans might be distinguished from God unconditionally. Within this distinction, human speaking about God would itself be unconditional. What I have seen in Luther's doctrine of God, in his Christology and his anthropology—if it is even proper to divide in such fashion—is always the same heartbeat, that is, that drawing of the proper distinction between God and humanity as a distinction for humanity's good. [19] This is what is meant to be learned and put into practice again and again. In a famous letter to Spalatin from Fortress Coburg (June 30, 1530), Luther thinks he sees even Melanchthon threatened by the dangers, sees that Melanchthon cannot properly distinguish between himself and God: "Be strong in the Lord, and on my behalf continuously admonish Philip not to become like God, but to fight that innate ambition to be like God, which was planted in us in paradise by the devil. This (ambition) doesn't do us any good. . . . In summary: We are to be men and not God, it will not be otherwise . . . ." [20]

But if the proper distinction between God and humanity gives to speaking about God the aspect which marks it as an unalterable, particular word, and as a word which applies to everyone unconditionally, then such an insight seems to me to facilitate a fruitful and fresh treatment of the pressing problem of so-called natural theology. A certain ambivalence in those texts of Luther which are usually pored over regarding this problem, and according to which everyone is able to be directed toward something like God, though without being able to verify the true God *remoto Christo* and *remota fide* (apart from Christ and faith), has always left me dissatisfied. In my judgment, we come further theologically when on the basis of that particular event of distinguishing between God and humanity *the nature of humanity* is formulated in statements which, of course, only the believer can identify as clearly beneficial, but which must still be recognized by unbelievers, thus apart from Christ and faith, as valid statements concerning human existence.[21] This is precisely the effect of that distinction between God and humanity which is given in the event of justification by faith alone. Even in the *Disputation concerning Man* (1536), Luther asserted that this event was not only a definition of the believer, the Christian, but quite emphatically a definition of the human being—of the "whole and perfect man. . . . Paul . . . briefly sums up the definition of man, saying, 'Man is justified by faith.' "[22] To be justified means to be unconditionally distinguished from God for one's own good. But for those who desire to be like God, such a definitive distinction takes on reality only when they no longer need to desire to become like God. And this occurs only when God is already nearer to them than they can ever be to themselves. But this nearness of God between me and me, as it were, can only be spoken of when it is essential that the human being be distinguished from itself.

This contradicts the current thesis that it is essential to humanity to become identical with itself. The contradiction is theologically necessary. I intend to make this clear by taking up the distinction between the inner and outer man* which is totally suspect today, but with which Luther worked in his treatise on Christian freedom.

Before turning to the fundamental theological distinctions in his treatise, I would like to relate at greater length how I learned to recognize and affirm Luther's skill (which merely *appears* to be formal in nature) in properly distinguishing as the consequence

---

*On the use of this expression, see the translator's preface, above, p. 12.

of his material, theological orientation. In this narrative, ideas from various writings will play a decisive role, especially some theses from the *Heidelberg Disputation,* a passage from *The Bondage of the Will* and from the extended treatises on the Supper, some formulations from the *Disputation concerning Man,* but also a single sentence from Luther's exposition of the 121st Psalm. They all orbit about the task of discovering the proper method of speaking theologically, the proper *modus loquendi theologicus,* in view of the indisputable invisibility of God.[23]

2

•

From the Invisibility to the Hiddenness of God

Ambivalence in the Invisibility of God

In his great debate with Erasmus, *The Bondage of the Will,* Luther reminds us of the New Testament statement that "faith has to do with things not seen" (Heb. 11:1).[1] Paradoxically, this reminder is appropriate for the reason that we cannot in fact see God. "No one has ever seen God" (John 1:18). The undeniable experiential fact that God is not to be seen must always be allowed to accompany all speaking about God. Whoever speaks of God without experiencing God's invisibility speaks past God as well as past his or her own reality. Then one should keep silent. But how and in what way does faith have to do with the invisible God? By itself, invisibility is an ambivalent phenomenon. God can be called invisible because he is unknown and cannot be experienced. In that case, to the invisibility of God corresponds his indeterminateness. Then the experience of God's invisibility would ultimately be the *experience that he cannot be experienced.* Our stance toward God would then have to allow for this capacity for experiencing that God cannot be experienced, either by arriving at a skeptical agnosticism, or (assuming that a certainty about God is still possible) by regarding human activity as expressing what is meant by the term "God." In the latter case—which actually is theologically relevant—the indeterminateness of God answering to his invisibility is remedied by the moral determinateness of human activity. The acting "I," addressable at the point of the distinction between good and evil, becomes something of a definition of God which guarantees his invisibility. Erasmus's position is at least within range of this view. And since many biblical texts can be quoted in terms of an "orthopraxis" which corresponds to God's invisibility, this view has been proposed again and again as a self-portrait of Christian faith: To "believe" means to act humanely. The humaneness of human life has the capacity for more clearly defining the God who in himself is indeterminate because he is invisible.

Luther, however, denies that this view has the right to offer itself as a self-portrait of Christian faith. For him, to believe in God means nothing else than just that—to *believe*. At first glance, this sounds tautologous. Yet nothing less than everything depends upon this apparent tautology. It asserts that *faith is irreplaceable*. For this reason, Luther in principle denies that the view he opposes can justifiably appeal to biblical texts. It is at bottom a "theology without a text." Its use of text is identical to dispensing with a text. In fact, this use of text is actually much worse than dispensing with biblical texts, because—whether consciously or not—it acts as though it were a theology related to the text, when it is not at all dependent on the texts it uses. But if Luther can have any significance at all for theology—in whatever present moment—then it is above all his reminder of theology's fundamental dependence upon the text of Holy Scripture to be interpreted. Fundamentally and to the very last, theology is exegesis. It is such, not in order *to use* Bible passages—on a suitable or unsuitable occasion—nor in order to concede a formal authority to Holy Scripture which would serve the absence of distinction and thus the absence of ideas in converse with biblical texts. One must rather "treat and deal cleanly with the Scripture. . . . False prophets go ahead and say, Dear people, this is God's Word. It

30

is true, and we cannot deny it. But we are not the people to whom he is speaking.''[2] It is not at all a matter of beginning something or other with the Bible, in order then to leave it behind. Rather, such a turn of phrase as "necessity forces us to run to the Bible,"[3] gives a clue to the proper understanding of theology as thoroughgoing exegesis. To live within the context of the biblical texts— highly diverse in subject matter and language—in order from there to shape and renew one's power of judgment ("to obtain there a verdict and judgment")[4]—this is the indispensable condition of theological existence, of which Luther reminded theology, something that really should be obvious and yet is clearly not obvious at all. To put it so as not to be misunderstood: Luther has no other significance than to be the bitterest enemy of a theology which does not metabolize by coming to terms with the Old and New Testament texts. Then, even the most learned Luther research can only function to reduce Luther's theological claim to the absurd. That is also something. But one should know what one is doing when one does it.

The Specific Hiddenness of God under His Opposite

Resorting to the theological context of biblical texts has its necessity. The "necessity" which "forces us to run to the Bible" is finally also the experience of God's invisibility. But this experience is not depicted as the experience that God cannot be experienced. It is rather the experience of being directed away from God's invisibility as *indeterminate* toward his invisibility as *determinate in a most specific sense.* Within the material context of biblical texts the indeterminateness of God which answers to his ambivalent invisibility is displaced by the highest possible degree of determinateness, so that in this context the experience of God's invisibility can become an experience of this displacement. Of course, even when "necessity forces us to run to the Bible," God can be experienced only as the invisible God. But in contrast to the ambivalent invisibility of a God who becomes definable primarily through human activity, within the material context of biblical texts God's invisibility can be experienced as the *specific* invisibility of his concrete hiddenness in the life and death of the man Jesus. It can be experienced as the invisibility of the God who has determined to be manifest under his opposite. *For this reason,* faith is related to "invisible things." For faith, which means nothing else than to believe, and thus which nothing can replace—not even the humanity of the human deed—can actually be defined as the human experience of the self-determination of God. So it is not true that faith in principle is related to the invisible, and *for this reason* is also faith in the invisible God. The reverse is true: The experience of God's self-determination to become manifest under his opposite constitutes faith as a relation to the invisible. On the other hand, under the (false) assumption of God's ambivalent invisibility, the Bible, its texts, would merely refer to an *absent* God, of whom we cannot say what he is, but at best only what he is not.

We may not underestimate the weight of this (false) premise. For me, Luther's significance for contemporary theology consists not least in the fact that he did not oppose to this premise (more prevalent today than ever) and its apparent plausibility an understanding of the Bible which construed its texts—or the utterances of the *viva vox evangelii* (the living voice of the gospel) in harmony with them—as references to an absent God, but as events in which God *as the absent One* is *present.* Still, the self-understanding of contemporary theology is largely dominated by that great tradition which could combine the need for the greatest possible particularity with the greatest universality in speaking about God in only a *negative* way. Thomas Aquinas, for example, made express appeal to the corresponding thesis of John of Damascus, that with respect to God "we cannot say what he is,"[5] and for his own part asserted that the "highest degree of human knowledge of God" is "to recognize that one does not know God."[6] "Now we cannot know what God is, but only what he is not. . . ."[7] This "Socratic theology," should one wish to compare its actual significance for contemporary theology with that of Luther, has indisputable preeminence. To the degree we encounter

32

the limits of human speech, with respect to the greatest universality[8] and the greatest possible particularity[9] in speaking about God, the ancient tenet seems to be confirmed that God is not definable, and that speaking about God which identifies him in a way that cannot be altered is actually impossible. In view of this dilemma all talk of God can at best be only silence made precise through speech. Now it is no longer speaking about God, but being silent about God which cannot be altered. But speech which can be nothing but the advocate of a silence which alone is appropriate moves on the boundary of resignation. But then, only one single, simple anthropological event, an event such as the modern discovery of moral autonomy with its corresponding human experience of freedom, is needed to plunge the unalterability of speech about God into doubt. Then theology becomes more and more a speaking about anything and everything, or it is speechless. This is the soil, this is the hermeneutical situation in which such remarkable phenomena as "theological atheism" thrive, an atheism which can only speak of the death of God— not, say, as giving final precision to speech about the living God,[10] but only as furnishing justification to leave off speaking about God.

In this situation, it seems helpful to me to let Luther remind us of the other, true significance of God's invisibility, and of the New Testament word which corresponds to it: "Faith has to do with things not seen." The *hidden presence* of God is the reason why faith has to do with things not seen. "He is not distant, but near you. . . . He resides in the midst of His Christians; there He is surely to be found. But He is not content just to dwell there. No, He also wants to be a God among them, a God to whom all hearts may flee, who freely gives all, does all, and is able to do all. . . . But this calls for faith. For the Father, the Judge, God, is present invisibly. His dwelling is holy; that is, it is set apart and can be seen only with the eyes of faith. If you believe that He is your Father, your Judge, your God, then this is what He is."[11] Not because faith brings this or that—and thus even God—

to light from out of universal invisibility, but because it participates in the hidden contemporaneity of God, since it enters into the material context of biblical texts as that movement which leads from the ambivalent invisibility to the precise hiddenness of God! In addition, Luther carried further his reminder that faith is related to the invisible to the point that all we believe must be hidden under its opposite. The result is that faith has a "situation in life" *(locus):* "It cannot, however, be more deeply hidden than under an object, perception, or experience which is contrary to it." [12] Luther then adds that this is sufficiently known from his writings.

A Creative View of the Hidden God

These ideas are sufficiently well known to the theology of our time. But if they are to gain *significance* for our own theological reflection, then this reflection would have to set out on the way which allows for a thinking about God which is not in spite of but, rather, due to his revelation as the invisible God. This will have to be a way which grasps the word which speaks of God as an event which neither avoids God's absence nor exaggerates it in the abstract, but rather allows God *as the absent One* to be *present.* [13] Finally, this way of thinking will involve making room for the vague experience of God's invisibility in such fashion that it can be conceived, not as the negative side of the visibility of this world and our perception of it, but as the most specific hiddenness of God *in* this world—a hiddenness made specific not least by the fact that the God who is hidden in the world can be experienced as the God who *for his part* is the *One who sees.* For if God for his part is the One who sees, then invisibility, even with respect to himself and his spiritual blessings, cannot be the last word. In his lecture on Ps. 121:3 ("He will not let your foot be moved, he who keeps you will not slumber"), Luther allows for the following terse dialog between God and experience fixed on the visible, or the insistence of reason *(ratio)* suited to it: "Reason says, I look at it in this way. But the Lord says, I see better than you." [14] This brief conflict-speech is more complicated than appears. Since Luther allows God to appear in this dialog as the One who sees better, the entire relation between visibility and invisibility is freshly defined. The visible world is not at all discredited. It is rather *seen together* with what the future holds for it and what is already evident to God's foresight. It is in his specific hiddenness that God becomes identifiable as the One who sees better.

This is true not only in respect of the general course of world history, but also—and inseparable from it—in respect of that peculiar occurrence within it. For ultimately God is the One who sees better insofar as he himself decides what should be *definitive* in whatever exists or occurs at any given moment. God sees better because his criterion is the finality and, in that respect, the definitiveness of all things. According to Luther, this definitiveness with which God himself sees is most intimately connected with that specific hiddenness in which God himself is manifest under his opposite. In dependence on a phrase (admittedly often misunderstood) in *The Bondage of the Will*,[15] we could also say that it is not the invisibility of the "God hidden in his majesty," but the specific hiddenness of the God who defines himself in his Word ("he has defined himself through his Word!") which constitutes the definitiveness with which God sees everything and for this very reason sees better in every respect.[16] But if we can construe God's superior power of perception not merely as a heightening of human foresight and the farsightedness which answers to it, but rather as a qualitatively different kind of perception by which what God sees first *comes into being,* then God's perception is by definition creative.

I would like to explain the extent to which this qualitatively different way in which God sees ultimately coheres with his own specific invisibility, and by referring to some of the "theological paradoxes" in the *Heidelberg Disputation.*[17] Its theses are at least oriented to the task of a theological definition of the relation between visibility and invisibility. The context gains clarity when we read the 20th and the 28th theses in parallel: Just as God becomes visible as the One hidden in suffering, just as he becomes knowable as the God hidden in the humiliation and shame of the cross[18] (since he wills to be *identifiable* as God only in the suffering and dying man Jesus), so he is related through love to his human creature, not by loving what is worthy of love or which delights the eye, but by loving its opposite, by loving what is altogether hateful in its sin and becomes worthy of love only through the love of God: "The love of God does not find, but creates, that which is pleasing to it[19]. . . . Therefore sinners are attractive because they are loved; they are not loved because they are attractive."[20] It is actually exciting to see how Luther (in contrast to the invisibility of God which the *theologus gloriae*—"theologian of glory"—seeks to know) gives expression to the specific hiddenness of God in the life, suffering, and death of Jesus Christ by means of the concept of the *visibilia Dei* (the visible things of God),[21] by an appeal to what is *visible* in God, and with that makes clear God's own being as an event which *in midst of* the visible world makes its way against the world. In so doing, he makes clear that it is precisely the God who makes his way in the visible world against it who seeks the advantage of the world. The distinctive trait of this "true theology and knowledge of God" localized "in the crucified Christ" is the event of love which "established at the cross" turns evil to good. "The love of God which lives in man loves sinners, evil persons, fools, and weaklings in order to make them righteous, good, wise, and strong. Rather than seeking its own good, the love of God flows forth and bestows good. . . . This is the love of the cross, born of the cross, which turns in the direction where it does not find good which it may enjoy, but where it may confer good upon the bad and needy person."[22]

The peculiarity of God's love, become identifiable in the cross of Christ, yields knowledge of what is distinctive about the divine perception. Luther removes God's love *(amor dei)* and love of the cross corresponding to it *(amor crucis)* from the structure of human love which from the outset arises from its object. He does so by explaining the character of human love on the basis of the character of human understanding. This explanation gives full clarity to that special quality in God by virtue of which he "sees better": The natural man cannot love after the fashion of the *amor crucis*. His *intellectus* (understanding) is not related to the *nothing,* but only to what is, to what is true and good. Accordingly, the human *intellectus* judges according to the visible appearance: "The intellect cannot by nature comprehend an object which does not exist, that is the poor and needy person, but only a thing which does exist, that is the true and good. Therefore it judges according to appearance, is a respecter of persons, and judges according to what can be seen, etc."[23] Conversely, what marks God's better sight is that it is directed toward the *nothing* (become articulable as such only in the shape of the crucifixion of Jesus Christ). Accordingly, within what is created, God's sight observes what is defined more by nothing than by being, more by absence than the total possession of possibilities. This divine sighting of the eye is superior, because *creative* love is at work in it, love which first creates its beloved counterpart by making it beautiful and worthy of love. Thus, wherever the gaze of the divine love is directed, an object of this love *arises* which is worthy of it. There, in God's eyes, and on this account also in actuality, the sinner, totally unworthy of love, crooked and ugly, becomes upright in a new righteousness and conformable to God. This creative power gives to the divine seeing its definitive character which passes sentence on whatever exists. The old saying, *ubi amor, ibi oculus* ("love opens the eyes"—and how it opens them!), takes on deepest significance here, insofar as the *amor crucis* opens the eye for what the nothing and nonentity are to become. Here, the traditional, metaphysical doctrine (reminiscent of Ps. 33:9) of the "original intuition," the *intuitus originarius*— by which, as Kant reminds us, "the existence of the object is given to the intuition," and for which reason it "can belong only to the primordial being"[24]—has undergone a transformation gained at the theology of the cross. Till now, the significance of this theology has been far too little observed or made use of, to say nothing of its depths having been sounded. A few implications should at least be indicated.

The Hermeneutical Consequence: Gaining a Metaphorical Language

Reshaping the old doctrine of the divine *intuitus originarius* (original intuition) by interpreting it in terms of the *amor crucis* furnishes a *modus loquendi theologicus* (theological mode of speaking) which has the tremendous advantage of allowing the basic *material* content of the Christian faith to yield results for the *hermeneutical* question regarding the possibility of appropriate speaking about God. The most intense concentration on the *Christus crucifixus* (Christ crucified) leads to heightening that power of perception which allows us to remain "true to the earth" in a theological way, and "to save the phenomena."

Here too a distinction must first be made. What was said of God's better power of sight applies analogously to the eye of faith—but not to reason's power of perception. The direction of reason's gaze is different. Just as only faith can see the God hidden beneath his opposite—for "through the only begotten Son and through the Gospel one learns to look directly into God's face"[25]—so faith, insofar as it sees God at work in the world, views the world in light of the Word of this God. Faith is therefore distinct from the perceptive power of reason, which by its own light sees what makes for the worldliness of the world: "In temporal things concerning man, man is reasonable enough; he needs no other light than the light of reason. For this reason God does not teach in Scripture how we should build houses, make clothes, marry, wage wars, travel with ships, or do such things so that they occur; since for that the light of nature is enough."[26] But the same natural light proves to be darkness when reason imagines it can know how "one pleases God and is blessed."[27] When reason perverts the task entrusted to it of knowing the world by presuming that "it is a service to God, when it really is not,"[28] then it confuses light with darkness. "For when it comes to engaging in divine things, that is, in things which concern God, so as to please God and make one blessed, reason is rigid as a stick and even blind."[29] In fact, for Luther idolatry is born when reason is so arrogant as to "set up" its own "crude darkness" in divine things "as a light, and will not allow it to be darkness. . . . See! From this comes all idolatry."[30] In contrast to scholastic tradition, which construes the natural light of reason as a "middle light"—which when compared with Jesus Christ as the eternal light functions as darkness, but by itself, "in itself is a light"[31]—Luther assigns to reason the power to explain, to *illumine* the world in worldly fashion. But that power must be identified as a power which altogether *obscures,* when it claims it can shed light even where the eternal light lightens and gives "the world a new appearance." It is rather the case that "where Christ is not present, there is darkness, however great and however brightly it may shine, and makes no room for some in-between thing invented by the late scholastics when they say that between darkness and Christ there is natural light and human reason."[32] Because faith sees the world with the eyes of the God who sees better, it clings to that illumination of the world which reason by itself cannot perform. To this extent, faith sees the world differently than reason can see it. Faith is oriented to the *new* which the world itself cannot produce, and which for that very reason is nearer to the world than it can ever be to itself.

Since faith gives rightful place to the illumination which occurs in the light of the gospel, and since it therefore gives heed only to God's Word and "sees no other thing," it sees itself and thus all else in the proper light:

In faith one must close the eyes to everything but God's Word. Whoever allows something else than this Word to appear before the eyes is already lost. Faith clings only to the Word pure and simple, does not avert its eyes from it, looks at nothing else. . . . So, when one is about to die, and death comes, and he sees where he is going, where he will take his first step, and the devil comes and shows him how horrible and awful death is, and on top of it all he sees God's judgment looming up—then the devil has won, then there is no help, as long as he has this before his eyes. If he were clever and acted in such a way that he allowed no other picture to take shape in his heart, if he clung only to this Word of God, then he would stay alive, for the Word is living. Thus, whoever holds to it must abide where the living and eternal Word abides."[33]

The believer sees the world and self with the eyes of the creative God who sees into the void. For this reason, in the midst of death faith perceives a new becoming. That this has important consequences for hermeneutics can be shown by the metaphorical character of the language of faith.

To Luther's statements, often cited but seldom thought through in hermeneutical discussion, belongs the 20th thesis of *The Disputation concerning the Divinity and Humanity of Christ*[34] (readily misused in fundamentalistic fashion). The thesis states that it is necessary and true that "all words take on new meaning in Christ, though they describe the same thing." Though the analogous statement of the need for baptizing ideas[35] makes clear that this thesis is to be understood in terms of the logic of speech, this statement also is too readily construed in purely edifying fashion. But to understand what is meant we need to recall the significance of baptism as a bath that drowns the old Adam, and from which a new person comes forth and arises. Just as Christian baptism permits and urges the distinction between one and the same "I" in the old and new person, through which the two enjoy no other continuity than that of the Word of God which creates from nothing, so in Christ the words of our language gain new meaning alongside the old, a meaning which allows us to assign a *new essence* to one and the same existing thing. Further, as Luther makes clear, particularly in his debate with Zwingli, he gives highest value to the fact that in such metaphorical usage the speech is not inauthentic, but truly authentic. "In such expressions we are speaking of an essence, what a person is and not what he represents, and we coin a new word to express his new essence," as the study of grammar teaches. "This art teaches how a child may make two or three words out of one, or how he may give to a single word a new application and several meanings."[36] So, for example, the word "rock," when used metaphorically—while retaining its own peculiar meaning *(eadem re significata)*—gains new meaning in the *event* of usage. Of course, this new meaning allows us to imagine a rock in a mountain range, but only to point away from it to the man of whom it is said that whoever relies on him has built upon a rock. The "regenerated term" discloses a new sphere of meaning. Or, when formulated from what is to be designated metaphorically instead of from usage, when a word is predicated of it in a new sense, it is given a new meaning. This innovative disclosure of new spheres of meaning occurs in all metaphorical speech.

As early as in his treatise against Latomus, Luther takes up the peculiarity of metaphorical usage in greater detail. While Latomus assigns to the same word several meanings which belong to it from the beginning—the actual debate concerned the understanding of "sin"—Luther proceeds from the single, plain meaning of the term *(simplex et univoca vox)*,[37] in order then to argue that such words are often used metaphorically. But the metaphorical meaning may not originally be assigned the word. In that case one would be dealing with a mere equivocation that would require listing in the dictionary as one more meaning for the same term. Metaphor, however, represents a new usage of the same term, in contrast to the customary usage fixed in the dictionary. The metaphor represents the event of innovative freedom in language. As a result, it discloses a new meaning over against the lexical meaning, and represents something else than a mere equivocation. On the other hand, if we were to identify this graphic (figurative) way of speaking as a lexical definition of the term, and thus cite as many words as there are metaphors *(figurae)*, the metaphorical way of speaking, that is, its innovative freedom, would lose all sense.[38] What kind of dictionary would it be, Luther mocks, which would have to list the innovations of metaphorical speech as actual definitions, thus, for the word *tunica* would have to list "shirt" as well as "onion skin" (due to a corresponding metaphorical use in the Roman poet Persius)?[39] "But what kind of dictionary will it be . . .? However, if you made proper meanings out of these excellent innovations, how would you ever stop?"[40] A Babel of tongues results[41] when as *many words* as possible are made of *one word*, rather than beginning where possible from one single, basic meaning and tracing the alternate meaning only to the metaphorical use of the same word (a matter of free choice, but not of necessity).[42] But if we begin with the single, plain meaning of a word, then the metaphorical use becomes a marvelous aid to memory and understanding, and a delight to the spirit. Luther himself is amazed that metaphorical speech has such "energy," that it can address and move one so "potently." "I don't know what sort of power images have that they can so forcefully enter and affect one, and make every man by nature long to hear and speak in imagery."[43]

Within the horizon of this universal characteristic of metaphorical speech Luther assigns to metaphor a specifically theological function which he then establishes Christologically. According to Luther, Paul's statement that God made the one who knew no sin to be sin for us[44] means that "Christ . . . is made sin for us metaphorically."[45] In this way, the basic meaning of *peccatum,* according to which sin makes one a sinner, is retained, but now it is used in the metaphorical sense: *Christ, this sinner* is distinct from all other sinners, since he himself committed no sin. When Christ is described as sin or sinner, without it being said of him that he himself sinned, the traditional rule is adhered to for forming metaphors *kat' analogon*,[46] by which the metaphor must reflect a certain distance from the thing usually denoted by the term ("since similarity is not identity"[47]): "Christ . . . is made sin for us metaphorically, for he was in every respect like a sinner. He was condemned, abandoned, put to shame, and in nothing different from a true sinner, except that he had not done the sin and guilt which he bore."[48] In this sense, that is, in terms of a *translatio* (a *metaphora*, or *epiphora*) *secundem similitudinem* (a transfer according to likeness), but not *secundem identitatem* (according to identity), the texts in Rom. 8:3[49] and Heb. 4:15[50] also speak of Christ's similarity with our sinful existence. But according to Luther, the *content* of such New Testament utterances goes beyond the metaphorical usage of the word "sin," since these texts state that our sin was *actually* transferred to Christ.

In a keen expression, Luther gives *ontical* relevance to the *grammatical* figure of the *metaphora:* "In this trope there is a metaphor not only in the words, but also in the actuality, for our sins have truly been taken from us and placed upon him, so that everyone who believes on him really has no sin, because they have been transferred to Christ and swallowed up by him, for they no longer condemn. . . ."[51] Paul dealt with sin in this sense in Rom. 8:3:[52] Since he *transferred* our sins to Christ and thus made him to be sin, God condemned sin by sin.[53]

Hence, we have to do with an *event of existence* when dealing with the *speech-event* of Christological metaphor. The *translatio verborum* (transfer of words) implies a *translatio rerum* (transfer of existing things). The grammatical *metaphora* is, so to speak, reduplicated in ontological fashion.[54] Luther uses the figure of the metaphor metaphorically—not, of course, to allow an inauthentic way of speaking to become even more inauthentic, but to show that through its ontological reduplication the Christological-soteriological metaphor is an authentic way of speaking, and of such kind that a transfer of existence already occurred is given decisive expression in the word-transfer which corresponds to it. But this makes sense only when in the person of Jesus Christ the God who opposes nothingness with being and from nothingness in turn creates new being is so at work that in the cross and resurrection of Jesus Christ the contrast between life and death, being and nonbeing yields results for new being and eternal life.

So then, the particular thrust of the *language of faith* within the general, hermeneutical feature of metaphorical speech consists in the fact that the view for the nothing directed by the *amor crucis* discloses an *absolutely new* sphere of meaning. Now the created, existing thing can be said to emerge *new ex nihilo,* and that also means that it points to the greatest of all imaginable contrasts, the contrast between death and life as *a contrast which has been overcome.* The *modus loquendi theologicus* which corresponds to the *amor crucis* is the mode of innovative speaking. To the extent that in all its expressions this mode connotes the contrast between life and death, God's holiness and our sin, being and nonbeing as reconciled and overcome, it discloses to this world an eschatologically new meaning which allows it to speak in a *definitive* way. As innovative speaking the *modus loquendi theologicus* is a definitive speaking. Plainly put, the criterion of proper theology would be whether it dares to raise the claim to be definitive as innovative speaking. It is most exciting to see how at this point Christology and the doctrine of justification conjoin in the hermeneutical problematic of Christian discourse. When pursued to its root, speaking of the God who sees better discloses a dimension of Luther's theology whose potential for significance in our time, a time so studiously linguistic, cannot be highly enough prized.

The Anthropological Consequence: Humanity as the Creature on Which God Builds

We can best reach clarity about this dimension of Luther's theology by way of so-called theological anthropology. Anthropology is itself a decidedly modern science.[55] Paradoxically, however, the growing inability to make definitive statements about humanity parallels its emergence as a separate scientific discipline. The more we know of humanity, the less we can say what it is. And the less we understand the nature of humanity, the more senseless existence as such appears. As representative of many analogous remarks, let me recall the famous words of Schelling:

> Far from man or his activity rendering the world intelligible, he is himself the most unintelligible, and drives me inevitably to the opinion that all being is accursed, an opinion handed down with so many agonizing sounds from ancient and modern time. It is he, man, who drives me to the last despairing question: Why is there something at all? Why not nothing?[56]

In our time, Ernst Bloch wrote:

> We do not know who we are. We do not know where we come from and where we are going. Both must always be thought of and attended to together.[57]

The so-called *problem of meaning* as discussed in philosophy and theology today is most closely linked to the experience of incomprehensibility and resignation respecting our ability to define humanity. Humanity cannot be defined, *homo definiri nequit*—this is the basic conviction of modern anthropology. And only on the basis of this conviction is the question even raised of the meaning of life, of existence. The question of meaning is raised only when it is felt to be lacking.

Theology must take note of this situation. It must fulfill its obligation within it, and not past it. It is obligated to speak definitively about humanity. Of course, it will feel especially obliged to give a historical account of the fact that modern man has inherited the God who in his glory was once regarded as indefinable—*deus definiri nequit!*—and precisely with regard to his indefinability. This might be linked to the fact that by false appeal to the mysteriousness of the revelation the thesis of God's indefinability allowed for a *specific* speaking about God as a merely *churchly* matter. But in the forum of *secular* debates, reason began to be most expressly silent about a God who could not be expressed: "He should . . . not even be thought of, since this is impossible," writes Fichte, in order in this way to satisfy the Godhead of God.[58] But if God is not even thought of, then it will be difficult to understand humanity on the basis of that which is over against the infinite God. But if humanity is no longer understood on the basis of that which is over against the infinite God, then in its very finitude it becomes incomprehensible and indefinable. As finite, humanity inherits the infinite God by conceiving itself instead of God as incomprehensible and thus as indefinable.

But the duty to explain historically such a genesis may not divert theology from the dogmatic task of retaining its innovative speech in definitive statements about human existence. In studying Luther's *Disputation concerning Man* (1536), I have learned that humanity is understood theologically only when its being can be regarded as properly defined: "Theology to be sure from the fulness of its wisdom defines man as whole and perfect."[59] At the same time, of course, how this defining is to be understood will also have to be decided. At any rate, for Luther humanity is not defined *per genus proximum et differentiam specificam* (according to its special class and specific difference), but rather by an event encountering it: "Paul . . . briefly sums up the definition of man, saying, 'Man is justified by faith.' "[60] Man, woman is thus defined as a creature of tension, of the most extreme tension between sin and righteousness, but in such a way that it is not sin but rather God's righteousness which renders the decision. But in view of the incontestable presence of sin—about which theology can scarcely still speak seriously today—this spells a further tension in which human existence is lived out, insofar as justified existence ("in becoming, not in being") is "still under construction," and only with the resurrection of the dead will be completed by God.[61] Thus, by an existence fraught with tension, an existence not possessed but awaited, "man" can be defined as "the simple material of God for the form of his future life."[62] Humanity is the creature on whom God is doing construction.

Naturally, such a definition requires a continual return to the construction site at which we must know what we are about when we intend to understand the process of construction, thus God's work of building upon humanity. And that definition requires working with those fundamental distinctions without which humanity as a creature of tension could never be spoken of. For this reason, I would like to call to mind theological discourse as discourse which draws distinctions, and by means of that treatise in which Luther, building on a distinction more or less shunned today, defined humanity as the creature on which God is building. The treatise is *The Freedom of a Christian,* with its distinction between the inner and outer man—a distinction eminently suited to interpret humanity on which God is building as the creature for whom God as the absent One can be present.

3
•
The Freedom of a Christian

What is a Christian? Luther's Thesis

Despite its brevity, Luther's treatise *The Freedom of a Christian*[1] claims to be nothing less than "the whole of a Christian life in a brief form."[2] Accordingly, the first sentence of the German version gives the basic understanding of "what a Christian is."[3] The lapidary expression concerning what a Christian is strikes one as dialectical. The dialectic is determined by the contrast between master and servant, or between freedom and servitude.

We do well to note from the very beginning the sociopolitical context of the terms freeman/vassal, lord/servant. We will thus recall the feudal—and not merely feudal but almost self-evident—correlation between lord and servant, as Aristotle classically formulated it: If there is a lord, then there is (also) a servant. And if there is a servant, then there is also a lord.[4]

When we understand how obviously the concept of a *lord* implied that of a *servant* distinct from and subordinate to him, then we can evaluate the *theological use,* the *usus theologicus* of these concepts in Luther's treatise. If the use of a word decides its grammatical sense,[5] then we are dealing with utterances here which have been promoted to the rank of *theological categories.* And not only the *individual* utterance, but even more the most tense relation between utterances within the compass of *theological statements of principle* has the status of a category. The theological statement of principle reads:

A Christian is a perfectly free lord of all, subject to none.
A Christian is a perfectly dutiful servant of all, subject to all.[6]

In contrast to the sociopolitical thesis that where one is a lord another must be a servant, it is at once striking that here the same person—and of course the Christian person—is both lord and servant. This is a concept of a free lord which radically alters the notion of lordship. The bold connection between lord and servant within the same subject seems decidedly dialectical. Luther himself says: "pugnare videantur"—both utterances "seem to contradict each other."[7]

Still, what appears dialectical can be resolved: "These two theses seem to contradict each other. If, however, they should be found to fit together they would serve our purpose beautifully."[8] What first appears contradictory finally agrees exactly. Luther points out this agreement through Bible quotations which make contrary statements about the human being. In appeal to a series of contrasting New Testament definitions of human existence rooted in the contrast between *spiritual* and *bodily*, Luther writes: "Because of this diversity of nature the Scriptures assert contradictory things concerning the same man."[9] But the New Testament is not merely *quoted*. By means of what is quoted—not the quotation!—Luther also constructs an argument. In order to show that the dialectic of Christian existence is not contradictory, he appeals to the Pauline distinction between *two* men in *one and the same I*. Echoing to some extent the Christological language—certainly the tradition[10]—of the ancient church, he can also speak of this distinction as the distinction of two natures in *one and the same* person: "Every Christian is of a twofold nature."[11] This basic anthropological distinction is expressed in various terminologies, of which that between *inner* and *outer* man has become the most effective.* Luther makes it a principle for dividing his treatise: "First, let us consider the inner man[12]. . . . Now let us turn to the second part, the outer man."[13]

---

*On the expressions "inner man" and "outer man," see above, translator's preface, p. 12.

This distinction is scarcely familiar to us today. We live in a world in which *everything* must be outward, so that "inner" is not only nothing more, but "inwardness" has actually come to denote a fatal dimension. The distinction between inner and outer has lost its status as a category of human existence: "In attending to nature, you must always see the one as everything; naught is within, naught without: For what is within is without."[14] What Goethe required merely for the study of *nature* now applies to humans who understand themselves more and more according to a nature which they can no longer observe without altering. So it is no surprise that in the modern period, and in quite a new way, the fundamental distinction between inner and outer man which should furnish the basis for the noncontradictory connection between freedom and service, lordship and servitude in the life of a Christian,[15] has rendered suspect Luther's understanding of freedom, his concept of faith and as a result all of his theology. He is not always named in polemic against the "degeneration" of Christianity into a "religion of pious inwardness." But he is in mind.[16]

Luther is in mind, though what is denounced as a religion of inwardness has little or nothing to do with his distinction between the inner and outer man.

Conversely, a more exact study of Luther's treatise raises a question which makes for considerable disquiet in the contemporary theological scene. The question is whether we can even say what a Christian is, thus what it is to be free before God, when we can no longer distinguish between the outer and inner man, which each one certainly is at any given moment. At any rate, Luther is convinced that "no external thing" can make the Christian "free or godly," for "his godliness and freedom . . . are neither bodily nor external."[17] But such a thesis makes sense only when it is possible to draw some distinction between external and internal. And that is proper only when such a distinction is necessary. The shared conviction of the philosophical and theological traditions in which Luther grew up was that the distinction between inner and outer man is both possible and necessary. In his own way, Luther let it be known *in what sense* this distinction is possible and necessary. The treatise *The Freedom of a Christian* is its classical illustration. Occupation with Luther's treatise is all the more rewarding, since it is suited to reduce current misconceptions about talk of the "inward man" by the fact that the genuinely theological meaning of the distinction between the "outward" and "inward man" is grasped in a new way. A preliminary, brief description of these misconceptions may be appropriate. It will further make clear to what extent the prejudice reflected in them dominates even where it is not made particularly explicit. I refer to the polemic of Herbert Marcuse, which really became known only through the so-called student revolution, as well as to the older criticism of Max Scheler, which has remained almost unknown.

Criticism of Luther's Thesis:
The Antitheses of Herbert Marcuse and Max Scheler

Few of the Reformer's utterances have been so misunderstood as the thesis that Christian freedom is "neither bodily nor external." Its appropriation by transcendental philosophy, and the abuses and vehement rejection to which it was subject betray the same misunderstanding, though, of course, in the rejection of it Luther's thesis was often identified with its "positive" reception, or, that reception was projected back into his thesis. On the one hand, the judgment was that "with Luther freedom of the Spirit first made its beginning," albeit actually only "in nucleus,"[18] and, of course, it is actually the critics of Luther's doctrine of freedom who assign to it a decidedly "anti-authoritarian tendency"[19] (primarily because of "the transcendent nature of Christian freedom vis-à-vis all worldly authority" rooted in "the absolute inwardness of the person"). On the other hand, "this terrible utterance" of Luther that " 'no outer thing . . .' can make the free Christian 'free or religious' " is censured as a statement by which "actual unfreedom is subsumed into the concept of freedom."[20] By "actual unfreedom" the critic quite obviously means the absence of *social* freedom. This assumes that with respect to what is external the "inner man" is at least less "actual." What is "actual" is in turn understood to be the context of *effective praxis*, so that the protest *against* Luther's understanding of freedom is that the freedom of the inner man which he affirmed is of course "always already realized when man begins to act."[21] "His freedom can never be the result of an action. . . . The true, human subject is never the subject of *praxis*. Thereby the person is relieved to a previously unknown degree from the responsibility for his praxis, while at the same time he has become free for all types of praxis: the person, secure in his inner freedom and fullness can only now really throw himself into outer praxis, for he knows that in so doing nothing can basically happen to him. And the separation of deed and doer, person and praxis, already posits the 'double morality' which, in the form of separation of 'office' and 'person,' forms one of the foundation stones of Luther's ethic."[22]

This is a criticism which gets at what is basic, and it deserves basic attention. We could cite many of Luther's statements which give further support to this fundamental criticism. I will name just one, a statement nearest in time to his composition of the treatise on freedom, and in which he identifies the concept of freedom with that of indifference, gleaned from mysticism.[23] Still, such a multiplication of texts is only too easily suited to stifle the basic debate with heaping up evidence *pro et contra*. That debate is oriented to Luther's anthropological distinction between the inner and the outer man. For this reason, it was not a happy solution when in his dispute with "Marcuse's Criticism of Luther's Concept of Freedom,"[24] a dispute which otherwise has such merit and is always assumed in what follows, Oswald Bayer rejected this distinction as "totally inappropriate to the situation it describes."[25] The evidence that with such terminology Luther follows Augustinian tradition,[26] or that because the "fanatics" had appropriated it he was later very hesitant about using it,[27] should not exempt us from disputing with Luther's critics at the very point where Luther himself seems to have initiated this criticism. And that point is precisely the anthropological distinction between inner and outer, brought so sharply to attention by Luther in 1520. Naturally, the theological situation signaled in that distinction need not be expressed in these terms. But we should reflect on what may be lost when this situation can no longer be expressed in these terms, due to the fact that the term "inner" has been demoted to a fatal category, used only to denounce unpopular theological positions. In any event, with this distinction Luther evoked effects and interpretations of effects which oblige us to inquire into his own intention. Once more Marcuse: "Luther's pamphlet *The Freedom of a Christian* brought together for the first time the elements which constitute the specifically bourgeois concept of freedom and which became the ideological basis for the specifically bourgeois articulation of authority: freedom was assigned to the 'inner' sphere of the person, to the 'inner man,' and at the same time the 'outer person' was subjected to the system of worldly powers; this system of earthly authorities was transcended through private autonomy and reason; person and work were separated (person and office) with the resultant 'double morality'; actual unfreedom and inequality were justified as a consequence of 'inner' freedom and equality." [28]

In an essay published in 1919, and bearing the characteristic title, "On Two German Maladies," [29] Max Scheler delivered a similar polemical interpretation of Luther's distinction between the inner and outer man. Though from the anthropological perspective it is a harsher attack than Marcuse's, it has been virtually ignored in theological discussion. I will refer to Scheler's essay at length, because through his polemic rather than through Marcuse's I can make clearer to what extent Luther's understanding can be of benefit to the contemporary theological controversy over freedom.

Max Scheler speaks of "German maladies" when referring to "what is far too uncritically trumpeted in ever new tones as the great blessing of German 'inwardness.' " [30] He calls the term *inwardness* "one of the most intolerable constructs in modern German usage." [31] Yet he is aware not only of a "history of false inwardness," [32] but also of "truly noble features of the German character and . . . truly lofty ideas of great German souls and thinkers"[33] which that history has unjustly claimed. Among other things, Meister Eckhart's talk of the *soul's foundation (Seelengrund)* and of feeling serves to illustrate what it is to which the propagandists of "German inwardness" *per nefas* (wrongly) make appeal. Thus Scheler is not intent on disputing an "inner life,"[34] but rather a "pure inwardness" which forgoes description and actualization "in the monstrously 'outward.' "[35] In its pretended purity, "pure inwardness" is in fact "false inwardness." For this reason, to preach a "sphere of 'pure inwardness' " is to hand on a pseudonym for an entire "series of human *defects, weaknesses, even vices* . . . , whose existence has brought to light no mean *social expedient* for the self-preservation of the neo-Prussian state system and its continuance as a class-state, of the coalition of junkers and heavy industrialists."[36] "Social democracy," of course, is also aligned with this coalition, at least to the degree it disguises "its hostility to religion by declaring it to be a 'private matter' or purely 'inward' concern."[37] In support of this charge, Scheler writes that "in the unutterable depths of 'pure inwardness,' the Spirit, ideas, deeds, and disposition, the sense for beauty and religion, Christ himself, become simply harmless, irresponsible, meaningless. And the more they become so, the more unchecked the love of power, class egoism, bureaucratic routine bereft of ideas, military training, blind impulse toward work and activity as well as a search for pleasure without taste and spirit can take effect among those who are not obliged to inwardness—to that sole luxury of those who serve and obey."[38] Praise of inwardness is unmasked as the German's "great life-deception."[39] The general appearance of the term—supposedly absent from classical German philosophy and literature, with the exception of Fichte—is due to a situation in which "the materialism of the external praxis of life became the universal form of national life."[40] Nevertheless, "German Protestant preachers, theologians, philosophers" are said to be the "particular hereditary tenants of 'inwardness.' " According to Scheler, what they teach is "for the most part already based on Luther himself."[41]

In order to verify his thesis, Scheler matches "pre-Protestant Germany" against the results of the Reformation. "Pre-Protestant Germany had described its interior life in great *visible* symbols. In essence, South German and Rhenish culture together with its ethnological supporters determined the face of Germany. Literature, domes, cathedrals, Germanic justice, and the old German city all reflect this harmony, this penetration of soul and world, inner and outer, form and content."[42] By contrast, the mere word *inwardness* is an ideal "which does not take into its meaning any *content* of ideas, any positive value, any indication of a power of reason, any activity of soul or spirit fixed on a goal. In a mere spatial parable it denotes a sphere of existence in which good *and* evil, true and false, what is meaningless and what is meaningful, repressed hunger pains and the most sacred feelings and dispositions can appear equal."[43] Luther's theology is ultimately held responsible for this very ideal: "It was in Luther that the German spirit first of all—and based on the *highest* values, values which shaped all others after itself—renounced suiting the inward to the outward, real world; renounced the *harmony of outer and inner.*"[44] The Germans' "free-soaring inwardness" thus "first" developed "on *religious* soil." Scheler laid this at the door of that "religious division of the German into a soul which stands with Christ on the sunlit mountain of the Lord—hidden in him by faith alone and free of works—and a fleshly body which languishes in sighs under the law, a law which for Luther was merely finite and which dances about in the 'pigsty' of the earthly (Luther's words)."[45]

In the manner of the various charges of an indictment, Scheler further lists "Luther's tender, mystical consciousness of grace; his heightened, exaggerated sensitivity to sin, which allows him to root it in the covetousness of man himself and not only in the consent of the will; his one-sided, familiar orientation to the inward by which he expresses all the higher values of the soul." As their "corollaries" (already explicit in Luther's "person and work") Scheler lists Luther's "passivity and quietism toward the condition of public morality," on the one hand, and "advice with

a strong Machiavellian coloration . . . in all questions of politics,"
on the other. Next are named Luther's denial of "the church's
visibility" and its "hierarchical structure, its institutional inde-
pendence and autonomy over against the state," but also "the
one-sided control of that art of inwardness—music." Even the
fact that later Protestant "servants" of the Lutheran church (of
necessity developing into a "state church") with respect to their
"social origins—quite different from the situation in England,
for example, or in the Calvinistic world—come largely from the
servant classes inclined to subjugation," is alleged to be one of
the "results of Luther's basic religious experience."[46] So, no
doubt, "the dangerous word of Wilhelm II, that the German is
'limited outwardly and unlimited inwardly' (the word originates
with Chamberlain)"[47] also belongs to Luther's subsequent effects.

Now, this is rather much all at once. And along with its in-
ventory, the indictment against the danger of Luther's basic distinction between the believing soul and fleshly body is not to be
mitigated when Scheler also denounces Kant's "dualism of the
homo noumenon and *homo phaenomenon* (man in himself and
man as perceived through the senses)—the former free, the latter
absolutely determined"[48]—as well as Schleiermacher's abstract-
ing of "religion from morality"[49] as the totally logical results of
that German inwardness which Luther inaugurated. For in such
distinctions and abstractions Scheler uncovers something that is
not only "tragic, touching," but "somehow also thoroughly des-
picable." Yet he thinks he observes how "in ever new ways the
German bourgeois was able to justify its political passivity and
perilous servility 'transcendentally,' " and "to make of it a *virtue*."[50]

What should we say to this? These are not so much portraits
of living history as death masks which Scheler has removed from
past history.[51] In any case, opposition to Scheler's criticism should
not allow his exaggerated polemic to lure it into making things
too easy for itself. Debate with Scheler's charge against that
"pure," "free-soaring," or simply "false inwardness," which he
diagnosed as the "German malady," is indispensable, and should

have for its theme his fundamental objection to "Luther's ideas and nature." His objection is to that—alleged!—diremption of *outer* and *inner* which first and above all results in that "false inwardness."

A positive thesis underlies this objection, and it reads: "only at the portal of the *deed* do the contents of life divide, and they retain the unity of the . . . *person*."[52] This, of course, is a formulation in *genuine* opposition to Luther's distinction between the "outer" and "inner man." For it is Luther's basic conviction that a Christian understanding of human being must seek the unity of the person elsewhere than "at the portal of the deed." For this reason Luther distinguishes human being in such fashion that it is not first of all the deed which turns it toward the outside and thus is viewed as the "portal" of existence. What enters into a person is what turns that person toward the outside. Hence, the "portal" of existence and the unity of the person are to be sought where a word is encountered by which one is rendered human, where a word by turning one inward also brings one out of oneself.

Humanity between God and World

Luther's distinction between the "inner man" and the "outer man" is linked to 2 Cor. 4:16, and interpreted by Gal. 5:17. The Latin version cites both Pauline texts. For Luther they function by making thematic the elementary anthropological tension in which one and the same "man" *is man:* "Though our outer (man) is wasting away, our inner (man) is being renewed every day. . . . For the desires of the flesh are against the Spirit and the desires of the Spirit are against the flesh."[53] Here the elementary tension determining the humanness of the human being is heightened to opposition. Opposition between spirit and flesh, inner and outer man should then help us to understand and confirm Luther's dialectic—these "two contradictory things" respecting the freedom and bondage of one and the same Christian person. First, the dialectic is confirmed in the above-quoted thesis. It informs us in a general way of the nature of the Christian—

56

according to the Latin version in an even more general way of the nature of human being: "Homo enim duplici constat natura, spirituali et corporali":[54] "Man has a twofold nature, a spiritual and a bodily one."[55]

This disclosure, then linked to the two Pauline passages, could encourage the notion that according to its spiritual nature the human being is a free lord of all and subject to none, while according to its bodily nature the human being is a dutiful servant of all and subject to all. In that case, we would be dealing with a variant of Platonic-Augustinian anthropology. It is in this sense that the exegete has often given Paul's reference to the inner and outer man positive reception, or has rejected it from the viewpoint of content as a dualistic obscuring of the Christian kerygma.[56] Luther's use of the distinction between the inner and outer man would then be only a favorite *modus loquendi,* which disguises rather than illumines the theological situation he meant to describe. But there is no doubt that Luther understood that distinction as an *appropriate* mode of theological speech.

Naturally, with this distinction Luther moves in traditional language.[57] The *vocatur* (is called) which introduces the distinction, gives evidence of that.[58] So, where his own usage is concerned, we may not ignore the rules of traditional (e.g., Augustinian and mystical) wordplay as regards the distinction between *inner* and *outer.*[59] Nevertheless, the logic of the subject matter within the treatise's train of thought, and Luther's deciphering of it in his use of words, allows us to recognize a type of theological utterance which is unique to him respecting the meaning of the distinction between the inner and outer man (and the more general distinction between *inner* and *outer*).

This uniqueness consists first in a total break with the traditional assigning of lordship or freedom to the inner, and bondage to the outer man. In fact, Luther says that this anthropological distinction between the spiritual and bodily nature, thus between "inwardness" and "outwardness," moves the Bible to speak in contradictory fashion "of the freedom and bondage" of one and the same subject: "Because of this diversity of nature the Scripture asserts contradictory things concerning the same man."[60] In total agreement with the tradition, Luther fixes the freedom of the Christian within the "inward spiritual man." However, just as he assigns human freedom *(libertas),* so also he assigns human bondage *(servitudo)* to the inner man. By doing so, he characteristically sets *libertas* in direct parallel with *iustitia* ("godliness"), and *servitudo* with *iniustitia* ("evil"): "It is evident that no external thing has any influence in producing Christian righteousness or freedom, or in producing unrighteousness or servitude."[61] The Christian, of course, has an outward, bodily "man," which may fare well or badly, may be "uncaptive" and thus free, but likewise "captive" and thus unfree. Yet of such "outward things," as Luther terms *all worldly* conditions and actualities of human existence, "none . . . touch either the freedom or the servitude of the soul."[62] Yet, the soul is human life in its relation to God, and as such desires to be distinguished from its relation to everything which is not God. *Therefore,* "according to the spiritual nature, which men refer to as the soul, he is called a spiritual, inner, or new man," while "according to the bodily nature, which men refer to as flesh, he is called a carnal, outward, or old man."[63]

We will understand Luther's distinction between the inner and outer man only when we grasp it within the horizon of a further distinction between God and world. The basic difference between God and world—and this means, between God and his creature— makes clear why according to the witness of Scripture one and the same human being can be involved in such fundamental contradiction, why in *one and the same* human being *two* human beings strive with each other: "Because of this diversity of nature the Scriptures assert contradictory things concerning the same man, since these two men in the same man contradict each other."[64] Now, of course, we must make clear to what extent the conflict between the outer and inner man does not occur as the distinction first suggests, that is, that the outer man represents bondage, but the inner man freedom.

We saw that the inner man is the anthropological point at which humanity's freedom and bondage are decided. This conception in Luther does not become clear solely on the basis of the fundamental difference between God and world. It suggests that we understand the *servant* as the one who is totally engrossed in the necessity for carrying on existence in the world, or who enjoys surrendering and yielding to it. And conversely, it suggests that we understand the *free lord* as the one who liberates or allows himself to be liberated (sacramentally) from this bondage, who despite the necessity of carrying on existence in the world is totally surrendered to God in it, using the world but only just using it, and taking pleasure in God alone. Such an understanding of the distinction between inner and outer man would be Augustinian. Then we would encounter echoes of Augustine in Luther even here. It is all the more important that within a train of thought filled with echoes of Augustine we lift out that motif which gives Luther's use of the distinction between the inner and outer man its particular theological point.

Humanity between the New and the Old

We come nearest this point when we begin with that idea of Luther in which he is most intimately linked to Augustinian tradition, but at the same time in which he distances himself from it in nuclear fashion, so to speak. To the malicious inference drawn from his doctrine of Christian freedom, that it is a good thing but does nothing,[65] Luther replies: "That would indeed be proper if we were wholly inner and perfectly spiritual men. But such we shall be only at the last day. . . . As long as we live in the flesh we only begin to make some progress in that which shall be perfected in the future life."[66] This statement may be taken in thoroughly Augustinian fashion, that is, if we construe the "not yet"—till the last day marked off from any total "interiorizing" of the Christian life—as representing the transitory, temporal world which passes away precisely because of its ontological structure. The ontological difference between *transitory* and *eternal* would then be a tension which determines Christian existence, as indicated in the simultaneousness of the various claims of the "kingdom of God" *(civitas dei)* and the "kingdom of the world" *(civitas terrena)*. "Now already" the "inner man" belongs to eternity, but basically he *always already* belongs to it.[67] But for Luther, the outer man *passes away*—together with the created world—not so much because of the ontological quality of transitoriness in everything outward, while by virtue of ontological participation in God's eternity the inner man would *remain*. The dialectic of inner and outer does not correspond to the dialectic of accidental transitoriness or transitory accident and abiding nature—as for example according to the famous epigram of Angelus Silesius: "Man, become essential. For when the world passes away, what is accidental falls away. Nature is what persists."[68]

For Luther, the fact that till the last day the outer man is simultaneous with the inner man but will then *pass away,* coheres with the fact that in a very precise sense the outer man has become *old* and thus deserves to be called an *old man.* Conversely, the inner man is man become *new* and to that extent also deserves to be called a *new man.* But this distinction between new and old which Luther from the outset used in parallel with the distinction between the inner and outer man cannot be explained solely from the fundamental difference between God and world. Rather, the distinction between the old and new man is *Christologically* conditioned.[69] And only from its Christological origin is it clear to what extent the inner man can be both free and unfree. We will thus have to explain the understanding of freedom as well as the concept of the "inner" man from the Christological origin of the new which requires distinguishing itself from what is old.

For Luther the relation to that Christological origin is effected through the Word and faith. "For faith alone and the Word of God rule in the soul. Just as the heated iron glows like fire because of the union of fire with it. . . ."[70] In discussing the power of the Word and the capacity of faith, Luther approaches the mystery on account of which one is addressed by God's Word and provoked to faith. We will follow his attempt at approaching it.

According to Luther, the relation of the anthropological distinction between inner and outer to the Christological origin of the difference between old and new is given in the gospel as the Word of God. "One thing, and only one thing is necessary for Christian life, righteousness, and freedom. That one thing is the most holy Word of God, the gospel of Christ."[71] The soul—this is the inner man, the place of decision respecting freedom and unfreedom, because the inner man, the soul, *lives* from the fact that "it has the Word of God."[72] But note that what is at issue is not the soul's word, but the *alien* Word of God. It is not a word which the soul speaks to itself, but a word which *addresses* it and—so we must conclude—*by this means* distinguishes inner from outer, the new from the old man. It is God's Word entering from without which first turns one inward and in so doing distinguishes that one as inner man from himself or herself as the outer man. But this also means that the inner man is constituted from outside the self. One comes to oneself from without, and to far greater extent from without than the outer man who—taken in the abstract—would be someone without externality. The purely outer man would never be outside himself and for this very reason would never come to himself. Precisely because he would always remain in himself, he could never come to himself. He would be—no man.

On the other hand, it is essential to one whom God's Word has turned inward *to come to himself or herself.* For it is essential to react to the Word of God which addresses one and in this way *to relate to oneself*—whether *believing* the Word of God or *not believing* it. Faith is thus the human relation to self which *corresponds* to the Word of God. It allows what the Word has to say to do its work, for "faith alone is the saving and efficacious use of the Word of God."[73] For this reason the rule applies: "If you believe, you shall have . . . if you do not believe, you shall lack. . . ."[74] This fundamental tenet of Luther can only be understood when we conceive faith as that attitude in which one totally relies on what is heard. Faith is the *efficax usus verbi dei* (efficacious use of the Word of God), which makes effective use of the Word of God appropriate to it.

But faith corresponds to the Word of God only because it gives honor to the truth. To believe means to consider the one whom one believes to be "truthful and trustworthy." [75] We cannot give anyone a higher honor, not even God. Thus to believe God means to regard the true God as "truthful and righteous." [76] Truth clearly desires that it be perceived as such and in this way be honored. One can thus do God no greater honor than to believe him. Conversely, unbelief is the greatest dishonor one can do to God, [77] for unbelief declares him to be a liar.

The Solemn Exchange: Humanity as Creature of Truth

Theologically, we cannot value highly enough Luther's recourse to the *truth* as the primal and abiding element in the fellowship between God and his creature. Here our experiences of reality encounter the experience of the God who is above all reality. Whoever relies on *God*, by definition has to do with *truth*, and with truth as a power which inexorably exposes as well as heals. In the prism of the truth Luther has allowed to be reflected the mystery of the incarnation and the "happy exchange" between God's everlasting nature and our lostness, an exchange occurring in the story of the incarnate Son of God. And he has clearly held that theological reflection on this exchange as an event of truth is indispensable. For Luther, in faith there first occurs the most solemn of all exchanges, in which God is declared and in which God declares one to be *truthful*. "When, however, God sees that we consider him truthful and by the faith of our heart pay him the great honor which is due him, he does us that great honor of considering us truthful and righteous for the sake of our faith. That we consider God truthful and righteous, this is righteous and truthful, and it makes us righteous and truthful, because it is true and right that God be considered truthful; which those who do not believe do not." [78] Without truth toward God one is not truthful and thus also not free. Only the truth can make one free. [79] But in the medium of truth the human being is both object and subject, when spoken to by an alien authority addressing it and by this authority speaks to itself.

That is, God's Word addresses us in such fashion "that you hear your God say to you how all your life and works are nothing before God, but, along with everything that is in you, must eternally perish."[80] Consequently, the one who by faith gives truth its due would have to despair of self. *Would have to,* if God's Word addressed us only with respect to what we made of ourselves. But it also addresses us with respect to what God for his part will make of us. For this reason the one who by faith gives truth its due must not perish. Faith cannot give the accusing law its due without giving the liberating gospel its due even more.[81] Through his own humanity God has *overridden* humanity's lost existence and thus overridden his accusing word through his liberating word, a word which faith must trust *all the more:* "But so that you come out of and away from yourself, that is, out of your corruption, he sets you before his dear Son, Jesus Christ, and lets his living, comforting Word say to you: You shall surrender to him with firm faith, and trust in him anew."[82]

But when the one to whom God has spoken is summoned by this address to "come out of and away from yourself," then the result is that the inner man can come out of and away from himself. It is obvious that he must do so, in order to come out of his self-incurred corruption. For our formulation of the question we assert first of all that the *inner man,* in total contrast to an "I" shut up in its "inwardness," can *allow himself to be called out of himself* and can actually *come out* of himself so as to become a new man.[83] It is the inner man who can abandon himself in order to enter into others and engage, even abandon them. When the gospel addressing him summons him to "surrender" himself to Jesus Christ "and to trust in him anew," then the inner man must be designed precisely for the purpose of going out of himself in order thus—with another!—to become a new man. The inner or inward man is the person turned inward by the accosting word, and in the event of this turning is turned away from the self. The inward man exists in that change from within toward the outside. For this reason he can be turned away from himself.

The outer man, however, cannot perform this act, in any event not without the inner (man). The outer man is, if you will, far less agile. He remains in himself wherever he goes. He is the old (man), and is always such. But the inner man is in becoming and to that extent the new man, who becomes old then and only then when he remains with himself. Then he *necessarily* becomes old. Then he would indeed be nothing else than a double of the outer man. If he remained with himself, he would kill his inwardness, that incomparable freedom of movement for leaving himself, in order instead to be fixed upon himself. As Luther can say in another context, such a man *fixed* upon himself would be a *homo incurvatus in se,* a man curved in upon himself, so totally fixed upon himself "that he uses not only physical but even spiritual goods for his own purposes and in all things seeks only himself."[84] This is true also of the inward man whose transformation has been ruined. He would be the *double of the outer man* who, by the very fact that the inner man becomes his double, takes on excess weight which unavoidably hinders him from being or becoming an outer *man* who *corresponds* to the true definition of the inner man. As the outer man's double the inner man is altogether unfree and renders the outer man altogether unfree.

In view of humanity's actual unfreedom the assertion that the inner man is able to go out of himself is first of all merely an abstraction which must take on concreteness. Christian preaching has to do with this activity. The assertion that the inner man can go out of himself is in fact an anthropological utterance with ontological relevance. Yet as an abstract generality it ignores the extent to which the inner man can forfeit—and de facto has always forfeited—the freedom of movement which belongs to him. In contrast, Luther proceeds from the fact that the inner man is always unfree, thus in fact already exists as the outer man's double, and thus hinders the outer man from corresponding to the true definition of the inner man. To this extent, Luther's anthropology is profoundly determined by the certainty that the inner man is theologically characterized by an unfree will *(servum arbitrium).* The inner man who exists as the outer man's double cannot at all be free lord of *all.* Rather, in the language of *The*

Bondage of the Will,[85] and with precise reference to what the heathen regard as highest virtue or the philosophers regard as best, even with reference to what is most admirable in him or which the world regards as honorable and good, the inner man is nothing but *flesh*. But this means that the inner man's freedom of movement appropriate to his relation to the world is not ruined by this relation. It is only through unbelief that the inner man becomes the outer man's double, thus through a negative relation to God. But since Luther always conceives the relation of humanity to God as a relation to God's Word, the one who forfeits freedom is the one who fails the *Word of God*. Without this Word one does not come out of oneself. It is the Word of God which enables the inner man to go out of himself. Only through the event of God's Word does the statement that the inner man (in contrast to the outer man) can go out of himself become concrete, free of the semblance of abstraction, and, in this concreteness, universally applicable. For, the inner man is man *called* out of himself. He is always such in concreteness as the man called out of his *lostness*.

But—to put it hypothetically—the inner man would be such even if he were without sin. For in essence humanity is the creature *addressed* by God and insofar sojourns *with itself* together with the Word addressing it and in the event of this sojourn is also taken out of itself. As one who sojourns with himself the man *turns* inward and *is* all the more *turned* toward the outside. But what is outer is not the dimension of the outer man, but rather the external existence of the inward man. As the one who sojourns with himself and is all the more turned toward the outside, he is the inner man, distinct from the outer, and as a result must preserve this *distinction* as *correspondence*. In everything he follows the *Word* of God which constitutes him a *creature of change*. As creature of change he is both worldly and spiritual—which means that his spiritual existence is not a duplication of his worldly existence. Rather, following the Word of God, it is *an existence underway in the world,* an eschatological wandering, which before all else makes him a historical creature.[86]

The "Happy Exchange":
Humanity as Creature of Change

Humanity is originally a creature of change, insofar as it is created by the Word of God. But it is truly a creature of change only insofar as it comes out from its lostness through God's Word, thus comes out of itself anew: There is nothing in heaven or on earth by which or in which the soul *lives* and becomes free than "the most holy Word of God, the Gospel of Christ."[87] Thus also "nature . . . of itself" *(natura per seipsam)* cannot banish one's servitude to one's own works and to the illusion of being saved by them.[88] It is all the more important that the Word of Christ be *rightly* preached. Added to this, the Word itself effects *the change* which frees one from oneself. So Luther emphasizes that "it is not enough . . . to preach the works, life, and words of Christ as historical facts." And it is not enough to preach "sympathy" with Christ. Rather, Jesus Christ must be preached so that "faith springs up from you and me and is preserved." This occurs when Christ is preached in such fashion "that he may not only be Christ, but be Christ for you and me, and that what is said of him and is denoted in his name may be effectual in us." This proper preaching of Jesus Christ "is done when that Christian liberty which he bestows is rightly taught."[89]

But when Christ is preached so that he works in us what is to be asserted of him, then it is clear that Luther can call the inward man the *new* man, and the bodily man the *old* man. For as certainly as the inward man is always set off from the outward man as the *new* man through the Word which addresses him, and as certainly as the turning inward and being turned outward in contrast to existence-by-oneself is the absolutely new, just as certainly the gospel which addresses the inner man who is the double of the outer man—but in this very shape *fixed* upon himself—is the event of change from old to new. For the gospel speaks of the being of Jesus Christ as the historical event of the "happy exchange." And in speaking of it the gospel gives the believer a share in that of which it speaks. The happy exchange occurring in the being of Jesus Christ is the genuine event of change from old to new and to that extent the event which makes the one who is unfree a free lord of all and subject to none.

Now we must explain this understanding of humanity as creature of change by stepping further back into the Christological mystery, and viewing it from what ultimately and actually supports it. In doing so, we must also make clear that the distinction of outer and inner man has a primary function and ultimate significance, a function and significance which renders the distinction indispensable even if we were to dispense with the terminology.

It is necessary to explain the Christological mystery because it alone makes clear the nature of faith. Earlier, in fact, we had the "happy exchange" in view when we interpreted *faith* as the "solemn exchange" between the one who confers honor on the truthful God and the God who confers honor on the truthful person, and when we understood this *mutual verification* as the needle's eye through which whoever deserves to be called a free lord of all must pass. Still, the previous argument, if it ended here, could scarcely avoid the misunderstanding that "*faith* alone" without any real foundation would effect salvation. Earlier, Luther had described the divine action by which one is declared to be truthful by God's Word as merely God's *reaction* to the homage paid him, and by which in believing God one regards him to be "truthful, godly, and just," whereupon God also declares such a one to be truthful, godly, and just. The suspicion lurks that this process takes place according to the rule of *do ut des* (literally: I give that you may give). That suspicion is reinforced by the juridically pregnant formulation of the Latin version.[90] Superficial understanding is only too easily facilitated by that notorious misunderstanding of the continually recurring expression, "if you believe, you shall have," and of the no less famous formula of the *fides creatrix divinitatis* (faith, creator of divinity). And if (by suspending the critical proviso that faith is not the creator of divinity with respect to God but only ourselves) we add the statement *immediately following* that "outside of faith God loses his righteousness, his honor, his riches, etc.,"[91] then it is easy to charge Luther's theology with a "preoccupation with the self," a reflex action of the believing subject making sure of its own subjectivity, aware of the "divine person" only as "a means to such self-assurance."[92]

Still, no less than a Karl Barth lent an ear to the reproofs of Paul Hacker,[93] and by way of Luther's concept of the *communicatio idiomatum* (communication of properties) suggested a link in their historical effects between Ludwig Feuerbach and Martin Luther.[94] Is it true, then, that the *honoring of God* determines the sense and significance of what the Word of God says? Is Luther's motto that faith alone decides one's relation to God to be understood from out of that great tradition given critical reflection as early as in Xenophanes,[95] and to which Augustine[96] gives shape in these words: "Whatever one prays to and honors is for him a God," or which Friedrich Schiller[97] recapitulates in his lapidary sentence: "Man paints himself in his gods"? What, then, does it mean: "If you believe, you shall have"?

The Basis for the Exchange:
God in the Person of Jesus Christ

The misconception that faith would be a power which creates *ex nihilo* is first of all contradicted by Luther's statement that it is in fact *true* and *just* that God is *truthful* and *just*. Only for this reason is it also true and just that one concede this to him and confess that he is truthful and just.[98] Faith thus relies on the reliability of God. Yet precisely for this reason it deals with the contrast between truth and falsehood, in fact between being and nonbeing. Whoever allows God to be true can do nothing else than convict oneself of deception. Over against God it is the liar who is *impossible,* who does not let God be true and thus reduces God and the self to a single act *ad absurdum.* For this reason, the *believer* who considers God truthful would actually be lost if he were to make himself the measure of all things. But faith knows that even now and above all God is the one who precedes our conferring of honor on him, and thus also precedes our faith. Whoever lets God be true cannot take only his own deception seriously, but also at the same time must take all the more seriously the fact that God *as the one who precedes* saves the one who is lost in deception, and thus, apart from any *do ut des* transaction, *has* made that one true. In faith the divine gift of truth, a gift *already given,* is verified. Faith does not constitute but receives and ratifies the "happy exchange." Apart from this the word "if you believe, you shall have" would be theologically senseless.[99] This becomes clear in a particularly beautiful way through the metaphor Luther uses to describe the soul's union with Christ. In conjunction with Eph. 5:30ff., he compares the union to that of bride and bridegroom, and in this context interprets faith as the "bridal ring" *(annulus fidei)* by which the bridegroom legally makes the bride's sins, death, and hell his own, acts as if they were his own and as if he himself had sinned.[100] Faith can ratify this union as a "happy exchange and conflict" only because Jesus Christ as God and man is the one who has neither sinned nor can sin and thus cannot die or be damned.[101] The bridegroom gives his bride a share in his glory, while conversely taking her shame upon himself. That sins, death, and damnation are "swallowed up"[102] in the being of Jesus Christ, that in fact the change implies a blessed "struggle" with the powers of destruction, at the end of which we may speak of a "most pleasing vision not only of communion, but of a blessed struggle and victory and salvation and redemption"[103]—this is possible only because God himself shares in this conflict. Only on the basis of the personal union of the man Jesus with God can it be said of Jesus Christ that "his righteousness is greater than the sins of all men, his life stronger than death, his salvation more invincible than hell."[104]

The freedom of a Christian which results from the soteriological union of Jesus with the "inward man" is thus ultimately grounded in the Christological unity of God and man. Only in this way does it become clear that freedom as an exclusively *divine predicate*[105] can and must now be claimed as a mark of the Christian. The assertion of Christian freedom assumes the active and

69

passive presence of God in human existence. Only under this assumption does faith in Jesus Christ have any meaning at all for Luther. Otherwise "Christ would be a poor Savior" and "himself would need a Savior." [106] And only under the assumption that God himself is present in the conflict with human sin and the allied powers of destruction ending in a *happy exchange* does it make good sense when Luther interprets *faith* which makes use of Christian freedom as a *fulfillment of the First Commandment*. This fulfillment must precede whatever works are required, though these too should praise God and confirm one's freedom. The distinction between faith and works, thus between the inner and outer man, stands or falls with faith in God's presence in the sphere of the human. The assertion that every Christian "has a twofold nature, a spiritual and a bodily one," and the corresponding differentiation of the same person into an "inner, or new man" and an "outward, or old man," [107] reflects, as it were, the union of the divine and human nature in the person of Jesus Christ. But in this union of God and man in the person of Jesus Christ faith itself does not at all play a constitutive role. The inner man can profit from his union with Jesus Christ, but only because the union of God with humanity and the resultant union of Jesus Christ with the sinner is altogether a *divine gift*. To believe means precisely to be able to allow oneself to be given something, to be able to receive. When, in regard to the Creator and his gifts, Luther describes the "flaw in human nature," that "it does not remember that everything is created and given, but wants to make of it an 'I have done it,' " then the theological rule drawn up against it in his exposition of Psalm 127 ("but it should read: I have received it, the Lord has given it. Not: man has made it" [108]) should apply all the more to the reconciler and redeemer become manifest in Jesus Christ.

Effecting the Exchange:
Jesus Christ as Person in Office

The same situation is repeated in Luther's statements concerning the titles and offices of Jesus Christ, characteristically linked to the doctrine of the personal unity of God and man. As God's firstborn, Jesus Christ is king and priest, without faith's assisting him to obtain these titles and offices. But faith *profits* from Jesus Christ's royal and priestly being, which Luther also interprets after the analogy of marriage law as a being which confers participation: "Just as Christ by his birthright obtained these two prerogatives, so he imparts them to and shares them with everyone who believes in him according to the law of the above-mentioned marriage, according to which the wife owns whatever belongs to the husband. Hence all of us who believe in Christ are priests and kings in Christ."[109]

Luther's combination of the doctrine of the two natures of Christ with the doctrine of his offices provides the deepest basis for his *theological* distinction between inner and outer man, and for his thesis of the freedom of a Christian which can only be expressed within the horizon of this distinction. If recourse to the unity of God and man in the person of Jesus Christ yields the "ontical basis" for the possibility of the happy exchange between the divine righteousness or freedom and human sin or servitude, then the Christological interpretation of the special status given in the Old Testament to the (male) firstborn whom God "set aside and reserved for himself,"[110] *activates,* as it were, the two-natures doctrine. Because Jesus Christ is "the true and only first-born of God the Father and the Virgin Mary," therefore he is a "king and priest, though spiritually."[111] He exercises his office as king and priest, "but spiritually"! The addition of the word "spiritually" makes clear why the anthropological distinction of inner and outer man is indispensable. In exercising his office Jesus Christ distinguishes himself from the visible exercise of royal rule and from the visible function of human priesthood. He distinguishes himself from earthly royal and priestly officeholders by the very fact that he does *not* retain his kingdom and priesthood as reserved for him alone.

According to the sociopolitical ideas prevailing till the end of absolutism, the significance of earthly royal rule is that the *one* as royal ruler is distinct from the *many* he rules. Among the many who are ruled there may be degrees of subservience, but over against the one ruler all are ruled. This concentration of rule in one and only one figure (despite the German provincial principalities, and in the motto *rex regnat sed non gubernat*—the king reigns but does not govern[112]—less contested than confirmed) was an ideal which promised to benefit also the ruled, as Homer and Aristotle affirmed: "Things should not be ruled badly. The rule of many is not good; let only one be ruler." [113] Analogously, earthly priesthood lives just by that distinction between priests and laity. To live as a priest is "far more excellent than being kings." [114] To this, for example, the letters of Bishop Ambrose of Milan, who dared to expel the emperor from the sanctuary, give their own impressive witness. In short, priesthood and kingship involve a "twofold honor" which belongs to the firstborn over all the others.[115] And just as all others share a common disadvantage over against the firstborn, so all others share a lower rank over against king and priest, whether as a nation of subjects or as people of a church.

But in Luther's conception, the point of Jesus Christ's royal rule and priestly office lies precisely in the *repeal* of that distinction between ruler and ruled, priest and lay. Jesus Christ shares his birthright "with all his Christians, so that through faith they too must all be kings and priests with Christ." [116] He *is,* as firstborn, both king and priest. But he *is* both in such fashion that he *makes* us kings and priests. And by making us such, he sets us free. Our freedom, of course, is "spiritual," but not at all because it is alien to reality in the sense of that eschewed inwardness. Rather, because it is spiritual it is a most powerful freedom. Luther deliberately interprets this freedom by means of the concepts of power or force: "See! What a precious freedom and power of Christians it is. . . . Now who can imagine the honor and lofty dignity of a Christian? Through his kingdom he rules over all things, through his priesthood he rules over God. . . ." [117]

This use of the concepts of power and force yields the touchstone for the necessity of distinguishing the inner from the outer man. Without that distinction it can be proved that all these fundamental assertions regarding the Christian faith would sink into extravagant meaninglessness. Then more than ever the dimension of what Luther along with the tradition calls "outward" and "bodily" would be irrelevant for Christian faith. Any theology which *directly identifies* the Christian's spiritual freedom and power with what relates to life in the world must face up to the question whether it does not—paradoxically—allow what relates to life in the world to become irrelevant for Christian faith, since any *direct identification* of the spiritual claim of the *libertas christiana* with worldly claims can only allow this spiritual claim to appear as an extravagant statement and hypertrophic assertion. Only when the assertion of Christian freedom is *not immediately identified* with those extremely valuable freedom movements in all spheres of our earthly existence, only then is there such a thing as a Christian contribution to freedom movements in which human life is continually engaged at all levels of existence, but without being able to assign progress toward a freer life with unequivocal superiority over the horrible regressions into unfreedom.

Nevertheless, Luther makes clear that this invisible, spiritual freedom and lordship is not an entity unrelated to the visible world, that for this reason there can be no talk of "the man who is enclosed in his inner freedom."[118] And he does so by means of the spiritual kingship of Jesus Christ which constitutes this freedom and lordship. The assertion that Jesus Christ rules "in heavenly and spiritual things" is immediately followed by the rejection of the possible misunderstanding that because it is not of this world[119] his kingdom is also not in this world:[120] "This does not mean that all things on earth and in hell are not also subject to him—otherwise how could he protect and save us from them?"[121]

So there is no question but that the rule of Jesus Christ extends beyond the worldly realm of solid "thingness" which obtrudes on us so unavoidably. Among those "things"—corresponding to the etymology of that term—absolutely everything is included which temporally and in its actuality is for that reason in dispute

73

and in the legal sense subject to inquiry.[122] Luther illustrates this anthropologically by the most painful experience of temporal life—death: "We must die bodily and none may escape death, so we must also be subject in many other things."[123] In fact, death is a particularly apt example of the problem to be dealt with. For if the rule of the risen Jesus Christ over the death of all were to be understood in directly bodily fashion, the believer could no longer die this death. Whoever interpreted Christian faith to mean that bodily death no longer existed for the believer could only maintain faith as an absurdity. The distinction between *spiritual* and *bodily, inner* and *outer, old* and *new* man resists this absurdity. According to Luther, the Christian as free lord is master of *all.* Not even death, that instance of temporal life in dispute, is exempt. The Christian is master of all, thus also and precisely of bodily life, in the sense that nothing can harm *eternally:* "Nothing can do him harm. As a matter of fact, all things are made subject to him and are compelled to serve him in obtaining salvation."[124] In this sense "even death and suffering" must "be subject . . . and serve him in obtaining salvation."[125]

Thus, there is an "objectively" and "subjectively" *altered orientation* of the entire person toward death, effected through Jesus Christ and faith in him. And it is this *alteration* of humanity toward itself and its destiny which is brought about by the distinction between inner and outer man, in turn based on Jesus Christ's own being and work. As the man *who is one person with God,* Jesus Christ, in contrast to all others, is the absolutely *new* man, the *rich* bridegroom who "takes the poor, despised, evil little whore to wife and frees her of all evil, adorns her with all blessings."[126] As the truly firstborn of God the Father by the Virgin Mary, Jesus Christ, in contrast to all others, is not only the uniquely royal man and high priest, but even more the king and priest who *turns toward* all human existence, making rulers of those who themselves are ruled, priests of those who themselves are lay.

This *turning* is an event in the world which compels us to see in it the distinction between old and new, bodily and spiritual, outer and inner. The unity of God with the man Jesus signifies that God has already come nearer to humanity than it can ever be to itself—in just the same way as the loving bridegroom draws *near* to the beloved bride. And the kingship and priesthood of Jesus Christ, by which he makes the believer king and priest, signifies that through his gospel and through faith God comes nearer to every believer than one can be to oneself. *This nearness of God,* this *interior intimo meo* (nearer to my most inward self)— to speak with Augustine[127]—constitutes the *theological* difference between *outer* and *inner.* When in Jesus Christ God comes nearer to me than I can be to myself, then, because at work in me he takes me out of myself I *am* an "inner" man, who as such can go out of himself and in that very act is a free lord of all and subject to none.

This occurs in faith. Faith effects the *meaning* of the distinction between the inward and outer man. Unbelief, by which the inner man chooses an existence which is a mere double of the outer man, renders meaningless *from within* the distinction between inner and outer man: "He, however, who does not believe is not served by anything. On the contrary, nothing works for his good, but he himself is a servant of all, and all things turn out badly for him."[128] Now—despite all the formal similarity—this is *not* the servitude of the Christian which Luther asserted at the beginning of his treatise when he wrote that "a Christian is a perfectly dutiful servant of all, subject to all."[129] Rather, the servitude of unbelief consists precisely in the fact that man—exactly for the reason that he remains only in himself, as though he were an outer man inwardly—cannot leave himself. But the believer goes out of himself, because of reliance on the God who in Jesus Christ has come nearer and become more inward than would ever be possible for him or her. If God is *in us,* then *we are outside ourselves.* To this extent "a Christian lives not in himself, but in Christ . . . , by faith he is caught up beyond himself into God."[130]

Now it is also clear why Luther attaches the two offices of Jesus Christ, his kingdom and his priesthood, so strictly to the Word of God—thus to the so-called prophetic office—so that he can actually write: "Nor was Christ sent into the world for any other ministry except that of the Word."[131] In fact, Jesus Christ *rules* through his *Word* and again, in *teaching* and *interceding,* makes use of his priestly office through the *Word.*[132] Through his Word he reaches us in such fashion that God concerns us *directly* and *unconditionally.* Whoever "clings" to the Word of God "with a firm faith, his soul is so totally joined to him that all the virtues of the Word become the soul's as well," so that this one "becomes a true child of God."[133]

This, then, is the "inner man": The one who exists in fellowship with God,[134] who *actually* experiences this fellowship as a fellowship of the *Word.* The distinction between the inner and outer man is the anthropological expression for the gospel's relation to reality and its experiential content. In making this distinction—and the tacit presupposition of Luther's argument is that it is theologically intelligible only when it is made; that for this reason it is *not* a matter of contrasting two anthropological constants—one has the experience of *becoming* something which one absolutely cannot *make* of oneself: God's child. Addressed directly by God's Word, that person is the *creature of change,* who by faith in Jesus Christ is in turn destined to become a *new* man, but who, *in opposition* to the Word of God which directly and unconditionally addresses and concerns him, can only be an *old* man, counterfeiting his inwardness from within. Such a man would in the negative sense be a servant of all, just because he does not use the freedom of the inner man to go out of himself. But in the positive sense the man becomes a servant of all by the fact that he does not remain in himself, but in believing goes as a free lord "beyond himself into God," in order to enter into the service of the neighbor from out of the freedom of God: "By love he descends beneath himself into his neighbor." Thus *as* a free lord he becomes the dutiful servant of all, who again does not live in himself, but as himself lives in the neighbor.[135]

The Meaning of the Exchange:
The Freedom of Humanity

The activity of love for which the new, inner man has been set free renders the outer man a special theme. But it does not give attention to the outer man as a theme to be treated separately. That would be abstract. The outer man can only be given attention in the concrete when the relation between outer and inner man is made the theme. But this relation is both that of conflict, as Luther had already set forth at the beginning of his treatise, as well as of conformity. Now it is necessary to deal with conformity, in which the conflict between inner and outer man is always included in the theme. But what concerns us here is the victory signalized in that conflict.

If *freedom for love* is altogether an event which takes place in and is decisive for the inner man, then love itself is necessarily expressed in activities which in themselves are always the actions of the outer man. The anthropological distinction now takes on relevance in the difference between person and work. Luther emphasizes that "it is always necessary that the . . . person himself be good before there can be any good works, and that good works follow and proceed from the good person."[136] This statement clearly identifies "the person" with the "inner man," for whom everything depends on the fact that he does not constitute himself. Correspondingly, the person does not constitute itself through its own deeds. The person becomes a doer only through love. On the other hand, the person is constituted by God's Word and the decision between faith or unbelief which corresponds with or contradicts that Word. But the free or unfree person—dependent upon the decision—is expressed in its deeds. And the medium of its deeds is the outer man. The inner man lives life not only as a hearer of the Word, but as a hearer of God's Word "he remains in this mortal life on earth. In this life he must control his own body and have dealings with men. Here the works begin."[137]

By himself the outer man is not at all inclined to do what is obvious to the believer. While out of thankfulness to God the believer's "one occupation" is "to serve God . . . without thought of gain, in love that is not constrained . . . he meets a contrary will in his own flesh which strives to serve the world and seeks its own advantage. This the spirit of faith cannot tolerate, but with joyful zeal it attempts to put the body under control [the German text reads, 'seize it by the throat'] and hold it in check."[138] Thus, as greatly as the inner man wants to do "freely, joyfully," and without thought of gain what pleases God,[139] so greatly must the outer man be ruled, in order to do what is commanded. It is precisely the function of the inner man to rule the outward man, to spur it on to an activity which corresponds to the faith of the inner man, so that the works of the outer man become deeds of love. In this fashion, the outer man intent on the deeds of his desire becomes conformable to the inner man, just as through faith the inner man has been made conformable to God: "Here he must indeed take care to discipline his body . . . and to subject it to the Spirit so that it will obey and conform to the inner man and faith. . . . The inner man . . . is created in the image of God. . . ."[140] And just as the inner man's conformity with God is mediated sacramentally through the being of Jesus Christ and his office, so Jesus Christ as *example* becomes normative if the outer man should be conformable to the inner man, and by this means conformable to God as well. If Jesus Christ freely made himself a servant, "so a Christian, like Christ his head," though "thus free from all works, ought in this liberty . . . to take upon himself the form of a servant" to serve his neighbor.[141] First and above all else, the outer man must have become an obedient servant of the inner man and to that extent of God. Only then can he become in unrestrained love the "dutiful servant of all" who is "subject to *all*."

It is beyond question, therefore, that Luther's distinction between an inner and outer man within the same person does not aim to disparage theologically the Christian's relation to the world for the sake of "pure inwardness" which, "free-soaring," remains for itself, an ideal which "does not take into its meaning any *content* of ideas, any positive value, any indication of a power of reason, any activity of soul or spirit fixed on a goal," as Max Scheler polemicized.[142] And, it is out of the question that our treatise leads to the justification of "actual unfreedom and in-equality . . . as a consequence of 'inner' freedom and equality," as Marcuse thought he had to assert.[143] The opposite is the case.

Luther's goal is precisely the reverse of what has been said of him. This is evident in his setting the conformity of the inner man with God in parallel to the conformity of the outer with the inner man. In both instances *an existence destined for corre-spondence* is involved. In a formal respect, then, we are dealing with a twofold relation of correspondence: the outer man is to be related to the inner man as the inner man to God. The distinctions seem to give a better grasp of the connection to be preserved. What is already clear from the formal structure of the relation of correspondence has material support in the fact that it is not only the inner man's relation to God which is Christologically me-diated, but that even the conformity of the outer with the inner man appears under the Christological signature. Of course, Luther assigns highest value to the fact that the correspondence of the inner man to God is solely God's work; that with its occurring the human being does not figure as a doer, but solely as a hearer and believer: "Nothing makes a man good except faith."[144] This conformity recognizes humanity merely as a recipient, which can give God nothing but the honor of first receiving itself from him. Hence Jesus Christ is at work without anything human added, if the inner man is to be conformable to the God who is free and is thus to be a free lord of all:[145] "Insofar as he is free he does no works."[146] As Luther in referring to Augustine is in the habit of putting it, what is at stake here is the sacramental understanding of the reality of Jesus Christ, of Jesus Christ as *sacramentum.*[147] But the same Jesus Christ, if he has been at work without our aid as *sacramentum,* now also intends to be recognized as our *exemplum* by calling those he has freed to discipleship. And for that purpose those who are freed must in turn become active. The hearer of God's Word must become a doer of the Word, faith thus active in love. And this occurs when the outer man is made conformable to the inner man, since the free lord of all who is subject to none becomes the dutiful servant and subject to all: "Insofar as he is a servant he does all kinds of works."[148] It is out of the question that according to this view of Christian freedom "Christ himself" is calculated to become "simply harmless" in the "unutterable depths of 'pure inwardness.' "[149] Throughout even the Christian's earthly life Jesus Christ is the formative power. There is a Christological stringency prevailing in this analogy of proportion, by which God and humanity, but also humanity and the world are strictly distinguished from each other and—precisely for this reason!—intensively linked to one another.

Thus, we do no graver injustice to Luther's intention than to dismiss his distinction between the inner and outer man and his assertion of the conflict between the two as advocating an anthropological dualism with a "double morality."[150] Rather, Luther's distinctions intend to preserve the connection which must be maintained between God, humanity, and the world from being misunderstood and misused as a connection *without a direction.* He is concerned with what establishes this connection theologically, a connection which cannot be set up in any way at all: "Good pious works do not make a good man, but a good man does good works. . . . Consequently it is always necessary that the . . . person himself be good before there can be any good works, and that good works follow and proceed from the good person."[151] Because humanity never can be the result of its deeds, the category of self-realization—at times so naively adopted by contemporary theology—comes under discussion only *per nefas.* Because the concept of reality[152] underlying this category ignores both humanity and God, Luther denies that the metaphysical or moral establishing of the connection between God, humanity, and the world is able to offer any Christian understanding of humanity between God and the world. Christian understanding lives from the fact that God cannot be managed. If we were to forgo distinguishing the inner and outer man—in whatever terminology—then humanity would have to be conceived as acting subject and in its activity as realizing itself. Then I am my deed. Then the one who does not act would perhaps be an interruption of the one who does, a breach in the *vita activa,* a pause which—presumably as sleep—may be necessary, but really should not be. Such a conception necessarily ends in subordinating humanity's relation to God to human action. To offset this, Luther must round out and discuss his statements concerning the outer man by treating the relation between person and work, "to know how far good works are to be rejected or not."[153] The best works are "no longer good" when they claim to constitute the human being. For in so doing they "blaspheme the grace of God."[154] Then God, like the world, is treated as a means to the end of human self-realization— or, since God cannot be an intelligible theme for the person whose self is realized through activity, is entirely ignored. In that case, worship of idols or atheism, superstition or unbelief appears to be the alternative.

By contrast, the theological distinction between inner and outer man gives to the connection between God, humanity, and the world an *irreversible direction,* an orientation which prevents understanding the human exclusively as actor. The self is not produced through activity, and cannot maintain itself in its being: "Before man is created and is a man, he neither does nor attempts to do anything toward becoming a creature, and after he is created he neither does nor attempts to do anything toward remaining a creature."[155] Prior to all activity the creature is to be regarded as being and becoming, which does not become what it is through its deed. The surety for this is the theological category of the inner man. It makes the ontological assertion that persons do not make themselves what they are, and thus cannot *acquire* themselves. And this is in fact the goal of all self-realization through activity, that finally I myself may have or possess myself. The goal of all self-realization is self-possession, having myself without restriction. And lastly, the *philosophical* distinction between inner and outer serves this goal, insofar as it promises those who are free of external obligations that they are no one's possession, but possess themselves without restriction. But Paul's reference to the inner man as rehearsed by Luther serves an entirely different purpose, that is, to deny that one could ever have oneself. Instead of possessing oneself one is rather taken away from oneself, is destined to be and to become. This is enough—in any event when we are what we become through God's grace. Through our acting we become possessors who desire something or much in order to be able to possess ourselves. Through God's grace we become those who believe and love. But in faith and love we who were once possessors become beings once more, and as such become those who are about to be, those on whom God builds. We are taken away from ourselves to our own best advantage. Just for this reason we are free for the neighbor, free for the service of works.

The Result of the Exchange:
The Service of Human Works

The definition of the *outer* by the inner man serves a dual function. First, it renders the person in its relation to self thematic, insofar as it speaks of the works "which a Christian does for himself."[156] But it likewise renders thematic the person in relation to *all* others on earth, for whose sake faith sets to work with joy and love— in the work of the freest service:

> A man does not live for himself alone in this mortal body to work for it alone, but he lives also for all men on earth; rather, he lives only for others and not for himself. . . . This is a truly Christian life. Here faith is truly active through love, that is, it finds expression in works of the freest service, cheerfully and lovingly done, with which a man willingly serves another without hope of reward.[157]

Luther is not a spokesman for the individualism of Christian life, but for the communal structure of the *vita christiana*. And this structure should in turn be shaped by Christ's example, so that from the abundance of the life of our inner man which we owe to him, we do "freely, joyfully, with all (our) heart" what pleases God.[158] Then we become a Christ for the other.[159] In terms of Romans 13 and Titus 1, the Christian fulfills even the social and civic obligation "freely and out of love."[160]

Thus, with regard to ethics and social ethics, Luther places highest value on the *unity* of the inner and outer man. Within this dimension, the freedom of faith *already won* should "live itself out." In fact, it should work itself out with regularity. But the unity of inner and outer man must always first arise, and in such fashion that within that unity the distinction assumed proves its productivity. This is the case in two respects.

First, the distinction guards against identifying the kingdom of grace and freedom with the earthly realm, an identification which ignores the resistance to God's good will. In fact, one can already trace this resistance in relation to oneself, insofar as the believer encounters resistance to God's grace "in his own flesh." One's relation to the world is no more without contradiction than one's very relation to oneself. For the "contrary will" which faith finds "in his own flesh" already has a specific relation to the world. That is, it "strives to serve the world." [161] To put it under control and hold it in check is clearly a task for faith which it pursues "with joyful zeal." But all the zeal in the world cannot disguise the difficulty of the task now expected of a person's *activity* and which claims the person totally as a doer.

This at once makes clear the other significance by which that distinction within the unity of inner and outer man must be preserved. It has as its theme the human being as the responsible subject of its deeds. This responsibility is all the greater, since through activity and the deeds or works resulting from it one is not in turn responsible for one's being as person. And here, that distance which is rich in connection and is opened up by the distinction between the inner and outer man—i.e., between being and what ought to be, [162] between receiving one's person and acting, between one's most intensive, not lifeless, but most vital passivity and widest activity—is strategic for an understanding of Christian freedom and with it for a theological understanding of human being as such. If by grace and faith the inner man becomes a person who corresponds to God, then this being is responsible only to God. Free of responsibility for the self, one is all the more responsible to God for what is *now* made of it.

Respecting human activity, the relation to self and the world implied in that connection-laden distinction between inner and outer man is set within the dimension of ultimate responsibility. Through activity the outer man in unrestricted relation to the world must be made to correspond to the inner man and thus—provided the inner man is in conformity to God *(conformis deo)*—to God himself. Luther's anthropological distinctions have their thrust in the *victory* of this correspondence within an existence marked by resistance to God's grace and to that extent by self-contradiction. "Therefore . . . love . . . makes us free, joyful, almighty workers and conquerors over all tribulations, servants of our neighbors, and yet lords of all." [163]

On the other hand, without those basic distinctions we would trivialize the self-contradiction within human existence and the world as well as the resistance to God's grace which it exhibits, and thus would lose the facticity of sin as a theme for theology. *Etsi peccatum non daretur* (as though there were no sin) is often enough the argument of a "theology" which proceeds in such fashion, if it does not prefer to explain the self-contradiction in human existence and the world simply as a *moral* deficit, and oppose to sin thus identified something like moral rearmament or political morality. In either case the Christian understanding of humanity is gambled away. By contrast, the distinction between the inner and outer man restrains the naive view that the kingdom of God could be directly identified with one of the kingdoms of this world. At the same time, by contrasting the inner as the new man to the outer and old man in such fashion that the old man is made to serve the new—"so that it will obey and conform to the inner man and faith" [164]—the distinction checks the defeatist view that where the course of the world is concerned the Christian is allowed to give way to a religious speculating *à la baisse* (for a fall, i.e., anticipating a drop in price). Conversely, "here a man cannot enjoy leisure." [165]

Here, in midst of contradictory earthly life, the goal is to celebrate *"with joyful zeal"* the reasonable service of an activity carried out in a "love that is not constrained," and for the welfare of those "people" with whom one must "deal";[166] so that one may "serve God joyfully . . . in love that is not constrained."[167] Where such deeds are absent, love and Christian freedom are also absent, and sin assumes the throne. Then it is necessary to preach law and gospel—and both!

> We are not to preach only one of these words of God, but both; we are to bring forth out of our treasure things new and old, the voice of the law as well as the word of grace. We must bring forth the voice of the law that men may be made to fear and come to a knowledge of their sins and so be converted to repentance and a better life. But we must not stop with that, for that would only amount to wounding and not binding up, smiting and not healing, killing and not making alive, leading down into hell and not bringing back again, humbling and not exalting. Therefore we must also preach the word of grace and the promise of forgiveness by which faith is taught and aroused. Without this word of grace the works of the law, contrition, penitence, and all the rest are done and taught in vain.[168]

Thus, just as law and gospel for all their dissimilarity are still so related that God's *grace* makes its way with their help, so the distinction between inner and outer man must assist the outcome of faith's freedom in unconstrained deeds of love which the world so urgently needs. The distinction between inner and outer man advocates neither a dualism nor the identity of "this world" and "the world beyond." Rather, it enables us in our anthropology to take seriously the fact that on earth there is "a beginning and a growing," but first and above all a beginning and a growing of the new "which shall be perfected in the future life."[169] Note well that the new is not fulfilled by human activity, because it is not at all fulfilled on earth. But this very insight necessitates activity in a world which is always old, so that in the way in which the world exists, always old despite all the changes, it can at least become the point of departure for a parable of the kingdom of freedom. Where this occurs, the light of promise from the conformity of the inner man with God falls on the conformity of the outer with the inner man, so that we may understand the entire relationship of correspondence as a still greater correspondence between the believer and God in midst of such great contradiction.

Relative to the societal structure of Christian life, the correspondence between God and the believer (which in midst of contradiction is at least beginning to be achieved in the here and now) has its earthly, worldly culmination in a common participation in the good things of God. Luther flatly sets up a rule of superabundance: "According to this rule the good things we have from God should flow from one to the other and be common to all." [170] Thus, just as the blessings of God flow into us from Jesus Christ, because he has put us on as if he had been what we are, so they should flow from us to those who need them. In this way, spiritual gifts are translated into earthly gifts, insofar as the outer man in correspondence with the inner man does exactly what is "necessary, profitable" to the other. What is necessary is *seen*[171] by the one whose inner eye is open: "I will therefore give myself as a Christ to my neighbor . . . , I will do nothing in this life except what I see is necessary, profitable, and salutary to my neighbor." [172] "Love's setting of goals and aspirations . . . are the result of nothing else than the analysis of reality, thus of the engagement of reason. . . . Those wakened to love have eyes, ears and gray matter; they see and indicate to one another the needs of their fellow human beings; they inquire after causes and methods of assistance, and in exchange love shows them the goal, certainly also for relationships in society." [173] This is indicated, for example, in Luther's other writings from the same year.

But the one who is free also sees the neighbor's *spiritual* need when inquiring in earnest about what "may be necessary, profitable and salutary." [174] Thus the transposing of God's abundant spiritual gifts into the dimension of earthly needs in turn benefits spiritual life. "The good things we have from God should flow . . . on to those who have need of them so that I should lay before God my faith and my righteousness that they may cover and intercede for the sins of my neighbor which I take upon myself and so labor and serve in them as if they were my very own.

This is what Christ did for us. This is true love and the genuine rule of a Christian life. Love is true and genuine where there is true and genuine faith."[175]

That faith may be genuine and abide—this is what Luther, if he ought or is able to mean anything to contemporary theology, placed once more on the agenda as its authentic concern and urgent task. If theology is responsible for reflecting on the truth of faith, then by such reflection it also leads toward responsible activity within the reality of life. But if it dispenses with responsibility for the truth of faith, in order instead to apply itself to those urgent and presumably more urgent problems of concrete and presumably more concrete life—as though the truth of faith were lifeless and abstract!—then, despite its preoccupation with the reality of life it is threatened with death. In such a situation, the recollection of Martin Luther's basic insights could assume therapeutic function. That recollection at least has diagnostic value.

In these reflections I have attempted to articulate the degree to which Luther could gain perceptible significance for contemporary theology, as that applies at present. In doing so, I have made rigorous selection. Such selection does not occur without arbitrariness. But if it is true that we must also draw distinctions within the Bible, this is all the more true—*ceteris imparibus* (other things being unequal)—of dealing with the Weimar Edition. In it too there is not a little which "does not apply to me, does not concern me." But "on that which does apply to me, I may boldly venture. . . ."[176] I have ventured. *Attemptavi. . . .*

Excursus:
The "Inner Man"

The oldest evidence known to me for distinguishing an inner
man *(ho entos anthrōpos)* from the outward form is contained in Plato's *Republic.* It appears in the midst of his
discussion of the question as to whether injustice profits the unjust
man if he is able to retain the semblance of being just (Plato, *The
Republic,* IX, xii, trans. Paul Shorey, LCL [1980], p. 399). Plato
gives his answer in the shape of a myth, inventing as a parable
of the soul one of those fabulous monsters which combines many
forms into one. He describes a manifold and many-headed beast—
partly tame, partly wild—to which a lion and a man are joined,
the three then forming one whole, and the outside molded into
the shape of one of them, the man, "so that to anyone who is
unable to look within but who can see only the external sheath
it appears to be one living creature, the man" (ibid., p. 401).
Whoever conceives injustice as profitable is led by the parable
ad absurdum, when insisting that feeding merely the composite
beast and the lion but not the man in the man is of benefit to the
man, when in reality it weakens him. "And on the other hand he
who says that justice is the more profitable affirms that all our
actions and words should tend to give the man within us complete
domination over the entire man *(hothen tou anthrōpou ho entos
anthrōpos estai egkratestatos)* . . . and caring for all the beasts
alike will first make them friendly to one another and to himself"
(ibid., p. 403). Here the inner man with the beasts within is
contrasted to the outward appearance of the man. In this fashion
the inner parts of this man represent the various parts of the soul,
its best part identified as the divine within, and whose mastery
over the other parts is also best for them—mastery does no harm

to the servant! (ibid., p. 404). When we note that in the same context Plato also describes the mastery of the divine element within the soul or inner man as the subordination of the desires to knowledge *(epistēmē)* and reason *(logos;* ibid., IX, xi, pp. 393, 395), then the Platonic distinctions appear to prepare the soil for a definition of the human as *zōon logon echon* ("having vital reason").

Plato's discourse on the inner man created a school. Plotinus later cites it expressly and interprets it in terms of his doctrine of the soul (Plotinus, *Ennead* V, 1, trans. A. H. Armstrong, LCL [1984], p. 47). According to that doctrine, the human being *hoion legei Platōn ton eisō anthrōpon* (which Plato calls the inner man) is one who exists apart from what is sensuous *(aisthētōn exō).* "Philo took it over from the heritage of Plato and sharpened further the dualistic aspect . . . dealing with it under the theme of the divine image. . . . In Paul and his school . . . it is varied through the eschatological antithesis of the old aeon and the new" (Ernst Käsemann, *Commentary on Romans,* trans. Geoffrey W. Bromiley [Grand Rapids: Eerdmans, 1980] p. 206).

Obviously, discourse on the inner man can be utilized from the most varied points of view, in any of which the idea of an ontological preeminence of the "man within the man" is dominant.

In later tradition the distinction between inner and outer man often seems to be a variation on the definition of the human being as rational animal. Both anthropological models are oriented to the idea of mastery over the self. Only by setting the two models in parallel does the assigning of freedom to the inner and servitude to the outer man become plausible. If we construe what is animal in the human being as an external quality linking it to the life-world of the beast, and on the other hand construe human rationality as an inward quality which rules what is animal and, through ruling, supersedes it, then we can in fact regard the distinction between inner and outer man as parallel to—if not the actual origin of—the definition which construes the human being as a rational animal. But then the reality of reason's capacity to supersede the animal appears to be the actual reality of life which supersedes the vitality of the animal—not through *heightening* its own life-force which is essential to it, but by *another quality* of life set over against that animal life-force, and from the outset superior to it (Aristotle, *Metaphysics* XII, vii, pp. 149, 151). Reason, this qualitatively superior reality of life, encounters in the human body as the organ of its earthly existence something external and as such repugnant to it, something it must first subdue, if it is not, as it were, to be taken captive and mastered by it. (In Plato as well the lower parts of the soul have a peculiar affinity for the body). From that external quality adhering to what is animallike in the rational animal, its reason *(ratio)* learns to understand itself as inward. The inwardness of reason is thus understood as its freedom for mastery over what is animallike within the rational animal and to that extent over the animal life-world as such. In this tradition—as early as in Plato's myth—the distinction between outer and inner man corresponds to one's encounter with the self in which the self is experienced as the encounter of two oppositely oriented realities. On the one hand, the self is experienced in what is most strange to it, in a "scarcely conceivable, impenetrable, bodily relation to the beast" (M. Heidegger, *Brief über den "Humanismus," Gesamtausgabe* I/9 [1976], p. 326), to the beast which one is accustomed to hunt, tame, ride, slaughter—in short, to make use of. On the other hand, the self is experienced in relation to reason. Due to its qualitative superiority over the animal life-world, reason is celebrated as a heavenly power, which then of course should be most rational and vital when—as a *noēseōs noēsis* ("a knowing that one knows")—it is exclusively concerned with itself. In this twofold relationship, fixed to a twofold origin, the self is experienced as the intersection of two realities, whose hostile conjunction moves one to distinguish in oneself what is outward from what is inward, and with a logical consistency to divide oneself into an inner and outer man. For metaphysics, it was this division which constituted the human being as that rational, living creature "who pursues intellectual activity, and who cultivates his intellect," who in self-encounter assists that part of the self to mastery which Aristotle described as "best and most akin" to the gods

(Aristotle, *Nicomachean Ethics,* X, ix, trans. H. Rackham, LCL [1962], p. 627). Thus, the rational animal is the creature destined for mastery over the self, in order thus mastered to rule the animal life-world as inanimate material. But since thought is *life* to the highest degree—pure, eternal life (cf. Aristotle, *Metaphysics* XII, vii, p. 15)—together with reason eternal life rules over the obviously transitory existence of the animal, which humanity also perceives itself to be. Because humanity is (rational) lord of itself, it also experiences that it is the (animallike) servant of itself. But when this relationship is reversed, so that the animal which we are enthrones itself as lord over the reason within us—when the lordship of reason within us over what is animal is only just threatened by it—then the outer man appears as prison of the rational soul. Then deliverance from that prison, at least through death, is the hope of the imprisoned inner man. And the entire life of the person intent on the lordship of reason becomes a study of death *(commentatio mortis).*

It is typical of the vastly different orientation in his understanding of the distinction between the inner and outer man that Luther addresses reason which should have the mastery so ironically as "Madam Reason"—"O domina Ratio."[1] The expression says enough. It is the place of absolute mastery which Luther denies to reason. Of course, Holy Scripture also understands reason *(ratio)* as mistress *(domina)* "super terram, volucres, pisces, pecora" (over the earth, birds, fish, and cattle).[2] And Luther can actually call it "omnium rerum res et caput et prae caeteris rebus huius vitae optimum et divinum quiddam" ("the most important and the highest in rank among all things and, in comparison with other things of this life, the best and something divine").[3] But that it should be one's master, that with reason one should master the self and be lord of one's sins,[4] is out of the question.

Notes

Foreword

1. This explains the frequent points of contact between this little treatise and that rather extensive book (*God as the Mystery of the World: On the Foundation of the Theology of the Crucified One in the Dispute between Theism and Atheism*, trans. D. L. Guder [Grand Rapids: Eerdmans, 1983]).

Chapter 1: The Question of Luther's Significance for Contemporary Theology

1. R. Wittram, "Die Zukunft in den Fragestellungen der Geschichtswissenschaft," in *Geschichte: Elemente der Zukunft,* Vorträge an den Hochschultagen 1965 der Evangelischen Studentengemeinde (Tübingen, 1965), p. 10.
2. *Enarratio Psalmi LI* (1532), WA 40/II, 327, 11-328, 9: "Cognitio dei et hominis est sapientia divina et proprie theologica, Et ita cognitio dei et hominis, ut referatur tandem ad deum iustificantem et hominem peccatorem, ut proprie sit subiectum Theologiae homo reus et perditus et deus iustificans vel salvator, quicquid extra istud argumentum vel subiectum quaeritur, hoc plane est error et vanitas in Theologia, quia non expectamus in sacris literis possessiones, sanitates corporum vel politicarum rerum, quae omnia tradita sunt in manus nostras et creata. . . . Ideo Theologia non pertinet ad hanc vitam, sed est alterius vitae, quam habet Adam."
3. Cf. *De servo arbitrio* (1525), WA 18, 605, 12f.: "unum aliquid assecutus, omnia assecutus" (*Bondage of the Will, LW,* 33:23: "If he had grasped one thing, he would have grasped all.")
4. *To the Christian Nobility of the German Nation concerning the Reform of the Christian Estate* (1520), *LW,* 44:205.
5. A. C. Danto, *Analytical Philosophy of History* (Cambridge, 1965), p. 111.
6. In fact, any theology could offer quite different "formulations of the question from our own point in time." Then we would not even be dealing with

common theological formulations. In contrast, by "formulations of the question from our own point in time," I mean what is fundamentally *in dispute* in theology.

7. Novalis, Heinrich von Ofterdingen, in *Schriften,* vol. 1, *Das dichterische Werk,* ed. P. Kluckhohn and R. Samuel (1977), p. 257.
8. The current and marketable discrediting of academic theology is still an ecumenical scandal, even though academic theology itself has greatly contributed to its falling into such great discredit as is presently paid it, especially in the so-called ecumenical dialog!
9. W. Maurer, *Von der Freiheit eines Christenmenschen: Zwei Untersuchungen zu Luthers Reformationsschriften* 1520/21 (1949), p. 25.
10. *Die Freiheit eines Christenmenschen,* 37, 1. The quotations follow the edition of L. E. Schmitt, *Neudrucke deutscher Literaturwerke des 16. und 17. Jahrhunderts,* No. 18 (1954³). In each instance, the reference is to page number and section (*LW,* 31:344).
11. *Freiheit,* 36, 1: "Sic et Christus, quanquam omnium dominus, factus tamen ex muliere, factus est sub lege, simul liber et servus, simul in forma dei et in forma servi" (*LW,* 31:344).
12. *Freiheit,* 37, 1 (the phrase does not appear in the English translation).
13. Thomas Aquinas, *Summa theologiae* I, q. 1 a. 7 crp: "Omnia . . . pertractantur in sacra doctrina sub ratione Dei" (St. Thomas Aquinas, *Summa Theologiae,* Latin text and English translation [London: Eyre and Spottiswoode, 1963], 1:26: "Now all things are dealt with in holy teaching in terms of God").
14. The reversal of this argument, that is, that because it speaks to everything and everyone theology aims at the whole and to that extent even amounts to a speaking about God, is, with all its self-raillery, the unconscious admission of its own lack of seriousness and the involuntary summons never to take it seriously. I note this because at the moment this reversal is not uncommon.
15. WA I, 225, 1f.: "Non potest homo naturaliter velle deum esse deum, Immo vellet se esse deum et deum non esse deum" (*Disputation against Scholastic Theology, LW,* 31:10).
16. *Operationes in Psalmos. 1519–1521,* WA 5, 128, 36-39: "Humanitatis seu (ut Apostolus loquitur) carnis regno, quod in fide agitur; nos sibi conformes facit et crucifigit, faciens ex infoelicibus et superbis diis homines veros, idest miseros et peccatores."
17. WA 19, 207, 3-6 (*Lectures on Jonah, LW,* 19:55).
18. *Operationes in Psalmos, 1519–1521,* WA 5, 128,39—129,4: "Quia enim ascendimus in Adam ad similitudinem dei, ideo descendit ille in similitudinem nostram, ut reduceret nos ad nostri cognitionem. Atque hoc agitur sacramento incarnationis. Hoc est regnum fidei, in quo Crux Christi dominatur, divinitatem perverse petitam deiiciens et humanitatem carnisque contemptam infirmitatem perverse desertam revocans."
19. In this respect I have not been able to detect any material difference between the "young" and the "late" Luther.

20. WA. B 5, 415, 41-46: "Tu esto fortis in Domino, & Philippum meo nomine Exhortare semper, ne fiat Deus, Sed pugnet contra illam innatam & a Diabolo in paradiso implantatam nobis ambitionem diuinitatis, Ea enim non expedit nobis . . . *Wir sollen menschen und nicht Gott sein. Das ist die summa; Es wird doch nicht anders. . ." (Letters, 1530, Selections, LW,* 49:337).

21. On the problem cf. W. Joest, *Ontologie der Person bei Luther* (1967), pp. 174f.; E. Jüngel, "Der Gott entsprechende Mensch: Bemerkungen zur Gottebenbildlichkeit des Menschen als Grundfigur theologischer Anthropologie," in *Entsprechungen: Gott-Wahrheit-Mensch,* Theologische Erörterungen (1980), pp. 291f.

22. WA 39/I, 176, 33-35: "Paulus . . . breviter hominis definitionem colligit, dicens, Hominem iustificari fide" (The *Disputation concerning Man, LW,* 34: 139); cf. WA 39/I, 176, 5f. The *Disputatio de homine* has been newly edited by G. Ebeling, *Lutherstudien,* Bd. II: *Disputatio de homine.* Erster Teil: *Text und Traditionshintergrund* (1977). The theses referred to here appear in that edition on pp. 22 and 19. Ebeling also indicates that when in contrast to Aristotle Luther takes up the definition of the *homo theologicus* (cf. thesis 28, ibid., p. 21), he does not have in mind "a particular type of person, for example, the Christian," but "rather the human being—every human being!—from a theological perspective" (ibid., p. 34).

23. In his excellent book, *Modus loquendi theologicus: Luthers Kampf um die Erneuerung der Theologie (1515–1518)* (Leiden, 1975), Leif Grane has correctly described Luther's theological work by means of this concept.

Chapter 2: From the Invisibility to the Hiddenness of God

1. WA 18, 633, 7: "Altera est, quod fides est rerum non apparentium" (*The Bondage of the Will, LW,* 33:62: "The second reason is that faith has to do with things not seen").

2. *Über das 1. Buch Mose. Predigten. 1527,* WA 24, 12, 14ff.

3. *Grund und Ursach aller Artikel D. Martin Luthers, so durch römische Bulle unrechtlich verdammt sind. 1521,* 7, 317, 5f. (*Defense and Explanation of All the Articles, 1521, LW* 32:11).

4. Ibid.

5. *Summa theologiae* I, q. 1 a. 7 arg. 1: "in Deo quid est, dicere impossibile est" (St. Thomas Aquinas, *Summa theologiae,* 1:25).

6. *Quaestiones disputatae de potentia,* q. 7 a. 5 ad 14: "illud est ultimum cognitionis humanae de Deo quod sciat se Deum nescire."

7. *Summa theologiae* I, q. 3 introd.: "de Deo scire non possumus quid sit, sed quid non sit" (St. Thomas Aquinas, *Summa theologiae,* 2:19).

8. "Deus non est in genere!" (God is not to be classified!)

9. "Individuum est ineffabile!" (What is particular is unutterable!)

10. Luther's concept of the doctrine of the communicatio idiomatum would of course suggest this. I have often argued that speaking of the death of God initially makes good sense Christologically, and to that extent is actually

indispensable to a legitimate theology. Cf. "Vom Tod des lebendigen Gottes," in *Unterwegs zur Sache: Theologische Bemerkungen* (1972), pp. 105-125; "Das dunkle Wort vom Tode Gottes," in *Von Zeit zu Zeit: Betrachtungen zu den Festzeiten des Kirchenjahres* (1976), pp. 15-63; *God as the Mystery of the World,* trans. D. L. Guder (Grand Rapids: Eerdmans, 1983).

11. *Deutsche Auslegung des 67. (68.) Psalmes.* 1521, WA 8, 8, 10-19 (*Commentary on Psalm 68, LW,* 13:6-7).

12. *De servo arbitrio.* 1525, WA 18, 633, 7-9. 13f.: "Ut ergo fidei locus sit, opus est, ut omnia quae creduntur, abscondantur. Non autem remotius absconduntur, quam sub contrario obiectu, sensu, experientia. . . . Qui nostra legerunt, habent haec sibi vulgatissima" (*The Bondage of the Will, LW,* 33:62).

13. Formulated in analogy to a table-talk of Luther, regarding the difference between philosophical and theological signs: It is necessary to understand this word not as a *nota absentis rei,* but as a *nota praesentis rei.* Cf. *Tischreden: Nachschriften von Johannes Mathesius. 1540,* WA.TR 4, 666, 8f., no. 5106: "Duplicia sunt signa: Philosophica et theologica. Signum philosophicum est nota absentis rei, signum theologicum est nota praesentis rei" (The philosophical sign is the mark of the absence of a thing, the theological sign the mark of the presence of a thing).

14. *In XV Psalmos graduum. 1532/33,* WA 40/III, 61, 5f.: "ratio: ego sentio. Dominus: ego melius sehe quam tu."

15. WA 18, 685, 21-24: "Caeterum Deus absconditus in maiestate neque deplorat neque tollit mortem, sed operatur vitam, mortem et omnia in omnibus. Neque enim tum verbo suo definivit sese, sed liberum sese reservavit super omnia" (*The Bondage of the Will, LW,* 33:140, "But God hidden in his majesty neither deplores nor takes away death, but works life, death, and all in all. For there he has not bound himself by his word, but has kept himself free over all things").

16. Cf. E. Jüngel, "Quae supra nos, nihil ad nos. Eine Kurzformel der Lehre vom verborgenen Gott—im Anschluss an Luther interpretiert," in *Entsprechungen: Gott-Wahrheit-Mensch,* Theologische Erörterungen (1980), pp. 227-232.

17. *Disputatio Heidelbergae habita. 1518,* WA 1, 353, 11 (*Heidelberg Disputation, LW,* 31:39).

18. Ibid., 362, 4-14 (*LW,* 31:52-53).

19. Ibid., 365, 2f.: "Amor Dei non invenit sed creat suum diligibile" (*LW,* 31:57).

20. Ibid., 365, 11f.: "Ideo enim peccatores sunt pulchri, quia diliguntur, non ideo diliguntur, quia sunt pulchri" (*LW,* 31:57).

21. Ibid., 362, 4: "Posteriora et visibilia Dei sunt opposita invisibilium, id est, humanitas, infirmitas, stulticia. . . ." (*LW,* 31:52, "The manifest and visible things of God are placed in opposition to the invisible, namely, his human nature, weakness, foolishness"). Cf. in addition L. Grane, *Modus loquendi theologicus* (Leiden, 1975), pp. 150f. The concept of the *posteriora Dei* (manifest things of God) contains an allusion to Exod. 33:23.

22. Ibid., 365, 9f., 13-15: "amor Dei in homine vivens diligit peccatores, malos, stultos, informos, ut faciat iustos, bonos, sapientes, robustos et sic effluit potius et bonum tribuit. . . . Et iste est amor crucis ex cruce natus, qui illuc sese transfert, non ubi invenit bonum quo fruatur, sed ubi bonum conferat malo et egeno" (*LW*, 31:57).
23. Ibid., 365, 17-20: "Cum tamen obiectum intellectus naturaliter esse non possit, id quod nihil est, id est, pauper vel egenum, sed entis, veri, boni. Ideo iudicat secundum faciem et accipit personam hominum et iudicat secundum ea quae patent . . ." (*LW*, 31:57-58).
24. Immanuel Kant, *Kritik der reinen Vernunft* (1787,[2] B 72.)
25. *Auslegung des ersten und zweiten Kapitels Johannis. 1537/38*, WA 46, 673, 8f. (*Sermons on the Gospel of St. John, Chapters 1 and 2*, 1538, *LW*, 22:157).
26. *Kirchenpostille. 1522*, WA 10/I.1, 531, 6-11.
27. Ibid., 532, 1f.
28. Ibid., 531, 23.
29. Ibid., 531, 11-13.
30. Ibid., 532, 14-16.
31. Ibid., 529, 4, 6.
32. Ibid., 528, 21-529, 2. The clarity with which Luther denies to reason the capacity for a proper knowledge of God is heightened by his conceding reason's ability to postulate the existence of a helper (!) God, without in fact being able to identify it as the existence of the true God, with the result that reason plays blindman's buff with God (*Der Prophet Jona ausgelegt. 1526*, WA 19, 205, 27-207, 14: *Lectures on Jonah, LW*, 19:55).
33. *Predigt am 21. Sonntag nach Trinitatis, 9. November 1522*, WA 10/III, 423, 17-21. 28-424, 4.
34. 1540. WA 39/II, 94, 17f.: "omnia vocabula in Christo novam significationem accipere in eadem re significata."
35. Cf., for example, the disputation on promotion of Palladius and Tilemann, 1537, WA 39/I, 229.
36. *Vom Abendmahl Christi: Bekenntnis. 1528*, WA 26, 274, 5-7; 271, 10-12 (*Confession concerning Christ's Supper, LW*, 37:173, 171.
37. *Rationis Latomianae confutatio. 1521*, WA 8, 83, 34 (*Against Latomus, LW*, 32:195, "the simple and univocal word").
38. Ibid., 86, 29f.: "Haec eo dicta putentur, ut probetur, scripturam esse refertam figuris, non tot significata et vocabula faciamus, quot fuerint figurae, alioqui quid opus figuris?" (*LW*, 32:199, "These things have been considered in order to show that Scripture is crammed with figurative language, so we ought not to make as many separate words and meanings as there are figurative expressions—for then what need would there be for such expressions?") Regarding the term *figura*, cf. also *Evangelium von den zehn Aussätzigen. 1521*, WA 8, 386-397, and *Dass diese Wort Christi "Das ist mein leib" noch fest stehen. 1527*, WA 23, 219, 15-28 (*That these Words of Christ "This is My Body," etc. Still Stand Firm against the Fanatics, LW*, 37: 109-110).

39. Cf. Persius, *Satire* IV, 30, in *Juvenal and Persius,* trans. G. G. Ramsay, LCL, p. 361.
40. WA 8, 84, 2-10: "Sed quodnam tum lexicon erit. . . . Et has egregias innovationes si velis proprias significationes facere, quis erit finis?" (*Against Latomus, LW,* 32:195-196).
41. Ibid., 84, 18f.: "Hinc natae illae aequivocationes. . . . sine causa et quaedam Babylonica confusio verborum" (*LW,* 32:196, "Equivocations arise in this language and a veritable Babylonian confusion of words").
42. Ibid., 86, 17-20: "Obsecro, . . . iustum autemne est tot vocabula ex uno multiplicare, cum possis vel omnia vel plurima in unum significatum colligere et figuris solis variare?" (*LW,* 32:199, "I ask. . . . is it right to make so many terms out of one when you can combine all, or most, into a single meaning and simply vary the figurative uses?").
43. Ibid., 84, 24f.: "Nescio enim, quae sit figurarum energia, ut tam potenter intrent et afficiant, ita ut omnis homo natura et audire et loqui gestiat figurate" (*LW,* 32:196).
44. Second Corinthians 5:21 obviously underlies Luther's formulation: "Christus dum offerretur pro nobis, factus est peccatum . . . " (Ibid., 86, 31f.; *LW,* 32:200, "When Christ is offered up, he is made sin for us . . .").
45. Ibid.: "Christus. . . . factus est peccatum metaphorice" (*LW,* 32:200, "When Christ is offered up, he is made sin for us metaphorically, for he was in every respect like a sinner").
46. Cf. Aristotle, *The Poetics,* xxi.7ff., 15ff., trans. W. Hamilton Fyfe, LCL, 1965, pp. 81, 85; *Rhetoric,* III.ii.8ff., trans. J. H. Freese, LCL, 1967, p. 355.
47. WA 8, 87, 2f.: "Oportet autem in metaphora aliquam differentiam esse a re vera, quia similitudo (ut aiunt) non identitas est" (*Against Latomus, LW,* 32:200, "However, in metaphors it is necessary that something be different from the real thing, because, as they say, similarity is not identity").
48. Ibid., 86, 31-34: "Christus. . . . factus est peccatum metaphorice, cum peccatori ita fuerit per omnia similis, damnatus, derelictus, confusus, ut nulla re differret a vero peccatore, quam quod reatum et peccatum, quod tulit, ipse non fecerat" (LW, 32:200).
49. "Misit deus filium in similitudinem carnis peccati" ("God . . . sending his own Son in the likeness of sinful flesh").
50. "Tentatum per omnia pro similitudine absque peccato" ("tempted as we are, yet without sin").
51. WA 8, 87, 6-10: "Et in hac translatione non solum est verborum, sed et rerum metaphora. Nam vere peccata nostra a nobis translata sunt et posita super ipsum, ut omnis qui hoc ipsum credit, vere nulla peccata habeat, sed translata super Christum, absorpta in ipso, eum amplius non damnent . . ." (*Against Latomus, LW,* 32:200).
52. "Et de peccato damnavit peccatum" ("he condemned sin in the flesh").
53. WA 8, 87, 28-30: "de peccato illo, quod Christum esse fecit translato nostro in illum, damnavit peccatum nostrum" (*Against Latomus, LW,* 32:201: "For the sin through which Christ was made sin [for our sin was transferred to him], our sin was condemned in him . . . ").

54. In the debate over the presence of Christ in the Eucharist, Luther repeats this hermeneutical-ontological thesis. To the merely verbal *alloiosis* ("change," "alteration") taught by Zwingli—and the tradition—which allows assigning predicates of Christ's divine nature to his human nature as an *inauthentic* way of speaking, Luther opposes an actual *communicatio idiomatum* by which a change in terms expresses a change in essence already occurred. Cf. for example, *Vom Abendmahl Christi. Bekenntnis. 1528*, WA 26, 319, 29-40; 321, 19-26; 322, 3-5 (*Confession concerning Christ's Supper, LW* 37:209-211); *Disputatio de sententia: Verbum caro factum est* (John 1:14), *1539*, WA 39/II, 12, 28f. (*Disputation concerning the Passage "Word Became Flesh," LW*, 3:272. Cf. in addition E. Jüngel, "Vom Tod des lebendigen Gottes," in *Unterwegs zur Sache* (1972), pp. 112-116.

55. Respecting its orientation, cf. O. Marquard, "Anthropologie," in *HWP*, 362-374.

56. F. W. J. Schelling, *Philosophie der Offenbarung*, Sämmtliche Werke, ed. K. F. A. Schelling, vol. II/3 (1858), p. 7.

57. E. Bloch, *Experimentum Mundi: Frage, Kategorien des Herausbringens, Praxis, Gesamtausgabe*, vol. 15 (1975), p. 239.

58. J. G. Fichte, *Der Herausgeber des philosophischen Journals gerichtliche Verantwortungsschriften gegen die Anklage des Atheismus*, Sämmtliche Werke, ed. J. H. Fichte, vol. 5 (1845), p. 266.

59. WA 39/I, 1765f.: "Theologia vero de plenitudine sapientiae suae Hominem totum et perfectum definit" (*The Disputation concerning Man, LW*, 34:138).

60. WA 39/I, 176, 33ff.: "Paulus. . . . breviter hominis definitionem colligit, dicens, Hominem iustificari fide" (*The Disputation concerning Man, LW*, 34:139).

61. *Promotionsdisputation von Palladius und Tilemann. 1537*, WA 39/I, 252, 8-15: "In fieri, non in esse. Interim dum hic iustificamur, nondum est completa. Est in agendo, in fieri, non in actu aut facto, nec in esse. Es ist noch ihm bau" (In becoming, not in being. However, while we are justified here, it has not yet been completed. It is in motion, in becoming, not in act or deed, nor in being. It is still under construction).

62. *Disputatio de homine. 1536*, WA 39/I, 177, 3f.: "Quare homo huius vitae est pura materia Dei ad futurae formae suae vitam" (*The Disputation concerning Man, LW*, 34:139: "Therefore, man in this life is the simple material of God for the form of his future life").

Chapter 3: The Freedom of a Christian

1. Despite the considerable literary attention given it of late, the treatise still has not found the commentary it deserves. Although H. J. Iwand made a first attempt, the same is to be desired for the treatise *The Bondage of the Will*, which is in particular need of a thoroughgoing theological commentary. I must confess that I do not understand what purpose is served by the entire mass of Luther research, when the foremost and profoundest task of an exegetical commentary on Luther's main treatises is patently not even perceived, to say nothing of being undertaken.

2. Translator's note: As indicated in chap. 1, note 10, the author's quotations are taken from the bilingual edition of L. E. Schmitt. These are then followed by the appropriate reference in the American Edition of *Luther's Works*. Thus here: *Freiheit*, 31, 16 = *LW*, 31:343.
3. *Freiheit*, 37, 1 (the phrase does not appear in English translation). The somewhat "more literary" introduction of the Latin version has instead the *Christiana fides* for its theme. Still, we will not err in the assumption that it is the *fides christiana* which makes the Christian a Christian. The thesis cited from the *Disputatio de homine* reads that the human being is defined as such by the *iustificatio sola fide*.
4. Aristotle, *The Categories on Interpretation*, 7, trans. Harold P. Cook, LCL, 1962, p. 55. Cf. ibid., p. 49, and *Politics*, 1:2, trans. H. Rackham, LCL, 1967, pp. 17, 19.
5. Cf. L. Wittgenstein, *Philosophische Untersuchungen*, 43, edited according to the bilingual text by G. E. M. Anscombe and R. Rhees, *Schriften*, vol. 1 (1960), p. 311.
6. *Freiheit*, 37, 1 (*LW*, 31:344).
7. *Freiheit*, 36, 1 (*LW*, 31:344).
8. Ibid.: "Haec quanquam pugnare videantur, tamen, ubi convenire inventa fuerint, pulchre facient ad institutum nostrum" (ibid.).
9. *Freiheit*, 38, 2: "Haec diversitas facit, ut in scripturis pugnantia de eodem homine dicantur" (*LW*, 31:344).
10. Cf. for example, Thomas Aquinas, *Summa theologiae*, I, q. 75 intr.: "Post considerationem creaturae spiritualis et corporalis considerandum est de homine, qui ex spirituali et corporali substantia componitur" (St. Thomas Aquinas, *Summa theologiae*, 11:3: "After created spirits and created bodies, man must be considered, a compound whose substance is both spiritual and corporeal"). In so doing, it is the theologian's concern "naturam . . . hominis considerare . . . ex parte animae, non autem ex parte corporis, nisi secundum habitudinem quam habet corpus ad animam" (to consider "human nature . . . by virtue of the soul, not of its bodily character, except so far as soul bespeaks embodiment," ibid.).
11. *Freiheit*, 39, 2 (the phrase does not occur in English translation).
12. *Freiheit*, 38, 3: "Primum autem interiorem hominem apprehendimust visuri" (*LW*, 31:344).
13. *Freiheit*, 58, 19: "Nunc ad alteram partem revertamur, ad externum hominem" (*LW*, 31:358).
14. Goethe, *Epirrhema, Werke. Vollständige Ausgabe letzter Hand* (1828), 3:96.
15. Luther's basic distinctions almost always have the function of maintaining and preserving a still more fundamental unity!
16. We will not mention here to what extent this polemic coheres with the Hegel renaissance, and thus with Hegel's interpretation of Reformation Christianity as a religion of subjectivity and of inwardness. With reference to Hegel, cf. his treatise, *Glauben und Wissen oder die Reflexionsphilosophie der Subjectivität, in der Vollständigkeit ihrer Formen, als Kantische, Jacobische, und Fichtesche Philosophie*, Gesammelte Werke, vol. 4, ed. H. Buchner und O. Pöggeler (1968), pp. 315-414, especially 316ff. According to

Hegel, the entire culture of the "modern period" is marked by "the color of the inner" (ibid., p. 412). The religion of Protestantism underlying this culture "builds its temples and altars in the heart of the individual" (ibid., p. 316).

17. *Freiheit*, 39, 3 (the phrase does not appear in English translation).
18. G. W. F. Hegel, *Vorlesungen über die Geschichte der Philosophie*, Sämtliche Werke. Jubiläumsausgabe, ed. H. Glockner, 19:254.
19. H. Marcuse, "A Study on Authority," *Studies in Critical Philosophy*, trans. Joris De Bres (Boston: Beacon, 1972), p. 53.
20. Ibid., p. 57.
21. Ibid.
22. Ibid., pp. 57-58.
23. In his exposition of Ps. 10:5, contained in the *Operationes in Psalmos*, 1519–1521, WA 5, 333, 23f., Luther denies that those who are righteous through works can be "homines omnium horarum, omnium operum, omnium rerum *liberi* scilicet et *indifferentes*" (men actually *free* and *indifferent* to all times, all deeds, and all things); emphasis added by the author.
24. Oswald Bayer, "Marcuses Kritik an Luthers Freiheitsbegriff," *ZThK* 67 (1970): 453-478.
25. Ibid., p. 472. Cf. this statement: "All throughout Luther is concerned to *distinguish* faith and love (within that unsuitable conceptuality of 'inner' and 'outer' man)," ibid.
26. Cf. U. Duchrow, *Christenheit und Weltverantwortung: Traditionsgeschichte und systematische Struktur der Zweireichelehre* (1970).
27. Cf. K.-H. zur Mühlen, *Nos extra nos: Luthers Theologie zwischen Mystik und Scholastik*, BHTh 46 (1972), pp. 272f.
28. Marcuse, "A Study on Authority," p. 56.
29. Max Scheler, "Von zwei deutschen Krankheiten," in *Schriften zur Soziologie und Weltanschauungslehre*, Gesammelte Werke (1963²), 6:204-219. The work was first published in 1919, then revised in 1923 and finally published in the collected works with the marginal notes inserted. It is possible that Marcuse was aware of this treatise.
30. Ibid., pp. 207f.
31. Ibid., p. 208.
32. Ibid., p. 211, this section partly in italics.
33. Ibid., p. 208.
34. Cf. ibid., p. 211.
35. Ibid., p. 209.
36. Ibid., p. 208
37. Ibid.
38. Ibid., pp. 208f.
39. Ibid., p. 209.
40. Ibid.
41. Ibid., p. 211.
42. Ibid.
43. Ibid., p. 209.

44. Ibid., p. 212.
45. Ibid.
46. Ibid.
47. Ibid., p. 211.
48. Ibid., p. 213. Scheler, of course, does not ignore the vast difference between Kantian philosophy and "Luther's ideas and nature": "The Kantian philosophy is in almost total contrast to Luther's ideas and nature. Luther's 'reason, the whore,' is for Kant the designer of the objective world of experience and the origin of all moral, religious, and legal order. 'You can because you should,' says Kant. Luther says, 'Do not suppose you already know where the moral law sets up an obligation' (*a debere ad posse non valet consequentia:* from 'should' it cannot logically follow that 'you can'). But the dualism between the *homo noumenon* and *homo phaenomenon*— the former free, the latter absolutely determined—between good 'intention' and action, morality and law is for Kant precisely *analogous* to the dualism of Luther between love and law, faith and work, the person who is a 'free lord' in Christ, and as a fleshly creature before the law is a 'slave' and 'unfree.' We should desire our neighbor's welfare, 'not as though something of his existence were of benefit to us,' summons Kant. That is, he summons us to will what we do not will, but at most desire 'within.' We should content ourselves with the formal, good intention of the will—quite indifferent to the content of our willing. Naturally, what most often results is that the subaltern or the official supplies the *content,* the changes in history, that is, in the territory of Königsberg! And since *only* the *content* matters to the subaltern or official, he leaves the 'good intention,' which by definition can be linked to *any* content, to whatever 'human material' he works with or commands. Thus each has what is needed: The intelligible 'I' in the unknown and unrecognizable sphere of the thing-in-itself has its good intention and can enjoy it at will in its inwardness—and at the same time whatever the subaltern wants occurs! It has been said that Kant's principle that a person may never be used as a means automatically excludes the militarism of the past. But the Kantian tenet reads: 'Not *merely* as means.' But why should the *homo = ens phaenomenon* not also be used as a *mere* means? The *homo = ens noumenon can* never lose his status. Kant has submerged this status so 'deeply' in inwardness that no worldly arm can reach it. The security systems were naturally different among Lutheran junkers than among Kant's Prussian burghers—but they reach the same goal" (ibid., pp. 213f.).
49. Ibid., p. 214: "The manner in which Schleiermacher in his *Religion: Speeches to Its Cultured Despisers* separates religion from morality, is opposed to Kant's moral theology. But for one who transposes Lutheranism into the forms of thought and feeling of Romanticism, the mere inwardness of religion only assumes a new shape" (ibid.).
50. Ibid.
51. Indeed, can a fundamental historical understanding ever do more than remove the death masks from history?
52. Scheler, "Von zwei deutschen Krankheiten," p. 211.

53. *Ei kai ho exō hēmōn anthrōpos diaphtheiretai, all' ho esō hēmōn anakain-
    outai hēmera kai hēmera* (2 Cor. 4:16). *Hē gar sarx epithymei kata tou
    pneumatos, to de pneuma kata tēs sarkos. . .* (Gal. 5:17).
54. *Freiheit,* 38, 2 (*LW,* 31:344).
55. *Freiheit,* 39, 2 (the phrase does not appear in English translation).
56. I cite examples which at times are taken from a context marked by his
    exegetical caution. In his *Vorlesungen über Neutestamentliche Theologie*
    (1864), p. 145, F. C. Baur writes: "In the *nous* . . . man is the reflective,
    self-conscious spirit; the *nous* is itself the *esō anthrōpos,* Rom. 7:22, the
    inner man, existing in his reflective self-consciousness." In his *Theology
    of the New Testament,* R. Bultmann remarks that in Rom. 7:22 and 2 Cor.
    4:16 Paul "uses the term 'the inner man' *(ho esō anthrōpos),* an expression
    that appears to be derived from the anthropology of Hellenistic dualism"
    (trans. Kendrick Grobel) (London: SCM [1952], 1:203). Cf. E. Käsemann,
    Perspectives on Paul, trans. Margaret Kohl (Philadelphia: Fortress, 1971),
    p. 16: In formulating his understanding of human existence, Paul "helps
    himself out with borrowings from Greek, sometimes using 'reason,' some-
    times 'the inner man,' thus coming close, at least, to a dualistic way of
    looking at things."
57. Cf. the excursus on pp. 89-92.
58. *Freiheit,* 38/39, 2 (*LW,* 31:344).
59. Cf. also K.-H. zur Mühlen, *Nos extra nos,* passim.
60. *Freiheit,* 38/39, 2: "Haec diversitas facit, ut in scripturis pugnantia de
    eodem homine dicantur" (*LW,* 31:344).
61. *Freiheit,* 38/39, 3 (*LW,* 31:344-345).
62. *Freiheit,* 39, 3 (*LW,* 31:345).
63. *Freiheit,* 39, 2 (*LW,* 31:344).
64. *Freiheit,* 38, 2: ". . . cum et ipsi homines in eodem homine sibi pugnent"
    (*LW,* 31:358).
65. We are reminded of analogous misconceptions of the great pointed remarks
    in Paul. Cf. for example, Rom. 3:5-8; 3:27-31; 5:20-6:2.
66. *Freiheit,* 59, 19 (*LW,* 31:358).
67. Let the reader recall the analogies with the anthropology of Philo and his
    traditions.
68. *Angelus Silesius, Cherubinischer Wandersmann,* ed. G. Ellinger, *Neudrucke
    deutscher Litteraturwerke des 16. und 17. Jahrhunderts,* no. 135-138
    (1895), p. 43 (Bk. 2, no. 30).
69. W. Maurer has most accurately evaluated the material context of the tractate:
    "Luther does not regard the person for itself alone, but in its union with
    and through Christ. For him, anthropology must be understood from the
    perspective of Christology. . . . The soul of the Christian is free of external
    things, not because of its spiritual nature, but as a result of the freedom,
    'die yhm Christus erworben und geben hatt' " (*Von der Freiheit eines Christ-
    enmenschen: Zwei Untersuchungen zu Luthers Reformationsschriften 1520/
    21* [1949], pp. 49f.).
70. *Freiheit,* 45, 10 (*LW,* 31:349).

71. *Freiheit,* 39-41, 5 (*LW,* 31:345).
72. *Freiheit,* 41, 5 (*LW,* 31:345).
73. *Freiheit,* 40, 6: "Fides enim sola est salutaris et efficax usus verbi dei" (*LW,* 31:346).
74. *Freiheit,* 45, 9 (*LW,* 31:348-349).
75. *Freiheit,* 47, 11 (*LW,* 31:350).
76. Ibid.
77. Ibid.
78. *Freiheit,* 47, 11 (*LW,* 31:351; the last sentence in the quotation does not appear in English translation).
79. In view of the current theological debates, we are forced to ask whether *truth* has any weight as a category in contemporary theology. Is it not true that theology is by far totally possessed with the questions, What results? Who profits? What is relevant?—and not by the question, What is true? Contemporary theology is predominantly at work under the leading category of efficiency, but not under that of truth. Not that we would advocate an inefficient theology! The concern is rather that a theology which aims at efficiency *instead* of inquiring into truth is intent on effects which are anything but effects of the truth. But in that case, another *freedom* is in mind than that for which the *truth* sets free.
80. *Freiheit,* 41, 6 (the sentence does not appear in English translation).
81. It is actually part of the truth of faith to confess that one cannot at all endure the extent of one's sin, nor even give a true definition of it: "Si homo sentiret magnitudinem peccati, non viveret uno momento, tantam vim habet peccatum. Quando vere sentitur, ut cum Nathan propheta dicit Davidi: Tu fecisti, ita territus est, ut iam quasi exspiraret, et procul dubio fuisset mortuus, nisi vocem prophetae audisset: Non morieris. Hac voce consolationem accepit et erectus est. Ex quo patet, et nos non intelligere veram peccati definitionem, sed tantum simulacra et ambigua" (Sin has such force that if a man were to perceive its extent he would not live for one moment. When he truly perceives it—as when Nathan the prophet says to David: You did it—he is so frightened that it is as if he were to die right now, and without doubt would have been dead if he had not heard the prophet's voice: You will not die. From this word he receives comfort and is lifted up. This makes clear that we do not grasp sin's true definition, but only images and uncertainties), *Promotionsdisputation von Johann Marbach. 1543,* WA 39/II, 210, 20-26.
82. *Freiheit,* 41, 6 (the sentence does not appear in English translation).
83. *Freiheit,* 40, 6: ". . . credens alius homo hac fide fieres" (*LW,* 31:347: "So that . . . you may through this faith become a new man").
84. *Römerbriefvorlesung,* 1515/16, WA 56, 356, 4ff.: "Et hoc consonat Scriptura, Que hominem describit incuruatum in se adeo, vt non tantum corporalia, Sed et spiritualia bona sibi inflectat et se in omnibus querat" (*Romans, LW,* 25:345).
85. WA 18, 744, 3-31 (*The Bondage of the Will, LW,* 33:228).
86. I note with pleasure that my understanding of Luther is most closely aligned

with the newer Pauline research. The reason for this, of course, must lie not only in the one who understands, but perhaps also in the fact that Luther himself was a Paul-researcher. "According to the apostle . . . (man) is a challengeable and a continually challenged being. This is a constitutive part of his existence. . . . Man is always faced with a call—a call to which he must respond in his thinking, his speaking, his acting and his suffering. He is a created being in that he experiences the divine address, which compels him to earthly pilgrimage. This fact makes him a historical being. . . . For salvation does not simply mean a state; it is . . . a path which is ceaselessly characterized by a forgetting of that which lies behind and a straining forward to that which lies ahead" (E. Käsemann, *Perspectives on Paul*, p. 5).

87. *Freiheit*, 39/41, 5 (*LW*, 31:345).
88. *Freiheit*, 66/67, 25 (*LW*, 31:363).
89. *Freiheit*, 56/57, 18: "Oportet autem, ut eo fine praedicetur, quo fides in eum promoveatur, ut non tantum sit Christus, sed tibi et mihi sit Christus, et id in nobis operetur, quod de eo dicitur et quod ipse vocatur" (*LW*, 31:357).
90. *Freiheit*, 46, 11: "Ubi autem deus videt, veritatem sibi tribui et fide cordis nostri se honorari tanto honore, quo ipse dignus est, Rursus et ipse nos honorat, tribuens et nobis veritatem et iustitiam propter hanc fidem. Fides enim facit veritatem et iustitiam, reddens deo suum, ideo rursus reddit deus iustitiae nostrae gloriam" (*LW*, 31:351: "When, however, God sees that we consider him truthful and by the faith of our heart pay him the great honor which is due him, he does us that great honor of considering us truthful and righteous for the sake of our faith. Faith works truth and righteousness by giving God what belongs to him. Therefore God in turn glorifies our righteousness").
91. *In epistolam S. Pauli ad Galatas Commentarius. 1531/35*, WA 40/I, 360, 5-7: "Fides est creatrix divinitatis, non in persona, sed in nobis. Extra fidem amittit deus suam iustitiam, gloriam, opes etc., et nihil maiestatis, divinitatis, ubi non fides" (*Lectures on Galatians, Chapters One to Four, LW*, 26:227, "[Faith] . . . is the creator of the Deity, not in the substance of God but in us. For without faith God loses His glory, wisdom, righteousness, truthfulness, mercy, etc., in us; in short, God has none of His majesty or divinity where faith is absent").
92. P. Hacker, *Das Ich im Glauben bei Martin Luther* (1966), pp. 23, 28, 53.
93. As indicated to me orally. But cf. also the letter of October 20, 1966, to Helmut Gollwitzer, in *K. Barth, Briefe 1961–1968*, ed. J. Fangmeier und H. Stoevesandt, Gesamtausgabe, Part V (1975), pp. 361f.
94. On the problem, cf. G. Ebeling, *Luther: An Introduction to His Thought*, trans. R. A. Wilson (Philadelphia: Fortress, 1970), p. 250, and "Was heisst einen Gott haben oder was ist Gott?" in *Wort und Glaube*, vol. 2 (1969), 287ff.
95. Cf. Diels-Kranz, *Die Fragmente der Vorsokratiker*, vol. I (1956[8]), pp. 132f. (21 B 15).
96. "Quod unusquisque colit et veneratur, hoc sibi deus est." Following a quotation in the Psalms commentary of Hugo Cardinalis—cf. G. Ebeling, *Wort und Glaube*, 2:293, together with note 17.

97. *Antrittsvorlesung*, Sämtliche Werke, ed. G. Fricke and H. G. Göpfert, vol. 4, (1968⁴), p. 755.

98. *Freiheit*, 46/47, 11: "Verum est enim et iustum, deum esse veracem et iustum, et hoc ei tribuere et confiteri, hoc est, esse veracem et iustum" (*LW*, 31:351).

99. So there is no more grotesque misconception than to denounce that celebrated, notorious formulation in Luther's Galatians Commentary (1531), that "fides" is the "creatrix divinitas"—"non in persona, sed in nobis" ("not in the substance of God, but in us," *Lectures on Galatians, Chapters One to Four, LW*, 26:227), as Luther at once takes care to add!—as a theological overstepping of the bounds or actually in terms of Feuerbach's thesis, that the deity is human perfection projected from out of man himself. The opposite is the case! For this very reason, according to Luther, God and faith belong "in one heap," since only faith can distinguish God and humanity in such fashion as God himself, in the event of his incarnation, distinguished himself from us for our salvation.

100. *Freiheit*, 48/49, 12 (*LW*, 31:352).

101. Ibid.

102. *Freiheit*, 49, 12 (*LW*, 31:352).

103. *Freiheit*, 48, 12: "Hic iam dulcissimum spectaculum prodit non solum communionis sed salutaris belli et victoriae et salutis et redemptionis" (*LW*, 31:351).

104. *Freiheit*, 48, 12: "Nam iustitia sua omnium peccatis superior, vita sua omni morte potentior, salus sua omni inferno invictior" (*LW*, 31:352).

105. Cf. also *De servo arbitrio. 1525*, WA 18, 636, 27ff.: "Sequitur nunc, liberum arbitrium esse plane divinum nomen, nec ulli posse competere quam soli divinae maiestati"; ibid., 662, 5: "ostendimus, liberum arbitrium nemini nisi soli Deo convenire" (*The Bondage of the Will, LW*, 33:68: "It follows now that free choice is plainly a divine term, and can be properly applied to none but the Divine Majesty alone;" ibid., p. 103: "We have shown above that free choice properly belongs to no one but God alone").

106. *Vom Abendmahl Christi, Bekenntnis. 1528* WA 26, 319, 38f. (*Confession concerning Christ's Supper, LW*, 37:210).

107. *Freiheit*, 39, 2 (*LW*, 31:344).

108. *In XV Psalmos graduum Commentarii. 1532/33*, WA 40, III, 223, 5-7: "Das ist vitium humanae naturae, quod non putat creationem et dona, sed vult ein feci draus machen; sed sol heissen: Ego accepi, Dominus dedit; Non: homo fecit."

109. *Freiheit*, 52, 15: "Quemadmodum autem Christus primogenitura sua has duas dignitates obtinuit, ita impartit et com[m]unes easdem facit cuilibet suo fideli matrimonii praedicti iure, quo sponsae sunt quaecunque sponsi sunt. Hinc omnes in Christo sumus sacerdotes et reges, quicunque in Christum credimus"; *LW*, 31:354).

110. *Freiheit*, 51, 14 (*LW*, 31:354).

111. *Freiheit*, 51-53, 14 (*LW*, 31:353-354).

112. On the formula *rex regnat sed non gubernat* cf. C. Schmitt, *Politische Theologie* II. *Die Legende von der Erledigung jeder Politischen Theologie* (1970), pp. 53ff.
113. Aristotle, *Metaphysics*, XII.x.14, trans. Hugh Tredennick, LCL (1962), p. 175; Homer, *The Iliad*, II.204, trans. A. T. Murray, LCL (1946), p. 65.
114. *Freiheit*, 55, 16 (*LW*, 31:355).
115. *Freiheit*, 51, 14 (*LW*, 31:353).
116. *Freiheit*, 53, 15 (the sentence does not appear in English translation).
117. *Freiheit*, 53/55, 15, 16 (these sentences do not appear in English translation).
118. Cf. Marcuse, "A Study on Authority," p. 57.
119. "Regnum enim eius non est de hoc mundo," *Freiheit*, 50, 14 (*LW*, 31:353).
120. Cf. *Freiheit*, 80: " 'Regnum meum non est hinc seu de hoc mundo,' ait Christus, sed non dixit 'Regnum meum non est hic seu in hoc mundo' " (*LW*, 31:373: " 'My kingship is not of this world,' says Christ. He does not, however, say, 'My kingship is not here, that is, in this world' ").
121. Freiheit, 50, 14: "Non quod non omnia etiam terrena et inferna subiecta sint ei (alioqui quomodo posset nos ab illis tueri et salvare?)" (*LW*, 31:353).
122. Cf. F. Kluge, *Etymologisches Wörterbuch der Deutschen Sprache*, ed. W. Mitzka (1963¹⁹).
123. *Freiheit*, 53, 15 (the phrases here and in the three notes following are not in English).
124. Ibid.
125. Ibid.
126. Ibid., 49, 12.
127. Cf Augustine, *Confessiones* III, c. 6, 11. CSEL 33, 53.
128. *Freiheit*, 55, 16 (*LW*, 31:355).
129. *Freiheit*, 37, 1 (*LW*, 31:344).
130. *Freiheit*, 79, 30 (*LW*, 31:371).
131. *Freiheit*, 40, 5: "Neque Christus ad aliud officium missus est quam verbi" (*LW*, 31:346).
132. Cf. *Freiheit*, 53, 14 and 55, 16 (*LW*, 31:354 and 355).
133. *Freiheit*, 45, 10 (this sentence does not appear in English).
134. W. Joest appropriately describes the person who affirms the essence of fellowship with God given to him and in affirming it exists as person an " 'enclitic' self," in contrast to the essence conferred on him. Cf. *Ontologie der Person bei Luther*, p. 376.
135. *Freiheit*, 79, 30 (*LW*, 31:371).
136. *Freiheit*, 63, 23 (*LW*, 31:361).
137. *Freiheit*, 59, 20 (*LW*, 31:358).
138. *Freiheit*, 59, 20 (LW 31:359).
139. *Freiheit*, 73, 27 (*LW*, 31:367).
140. *Freiheit*, 58, 20: "hic certe curandum, ut corpus . . . spiritui subdatur ut homini interiori et fidei obediat et conformis sit. . . . Interior enim homo conformis deo. . ." (*LW*, 31:358-359).

141. *Freiheit*, 71, 27 (*LW*, 31:366).
142. Cf. p. 53 above.
143. Cf. p. 52 above.
144. *Freiheit*, 65, 24 (*LW*, 31:362).
145. The cooperation of Christians in the proclamation of God's Word lies at an entirely different level. In this respect, Luther together with Paul describes the believers as *cooperatores*. Cf. *De servo arbitrio*. *1525*, WA 18, 695, 23ff. and 753, 20ff. *The Bondage of the Will, LW*, 33:154-155, and 242).
146. *Freiheit*, 59, 19 (*LW*, 31:358).
147. Cf. Augustine, *De trinitate* IV, c. 3 n. 6, CChr. SL vol. 50 (1968), p. 167 with WA 9, 18ff.; 56, 321, 22-322, 9; 1, 309, 16ff., 337, 13ff.; 2, 141, 11f.; 9, 440f.; 10/I 1, 10, 20-12, 3; 39/I, 356, 35ff. and elsewhere.
148. *Freiheit*, 59, 19 (*LW*, 31:358).
149. Cf. p. 53 above.
150. Cf. p. 51 above.
151. *Freiheit*, 63, 23 (LW. 31:361).
152. Cf. E. Jüngel, "Die Welt als Möglichkeit und Wirklichkeit: Zum ontologischen Ansatz der Rechtfertigungslehre," in *Unterwegs zur Sache: Theologische Bemerkungen* (1972), pp. 206-233.
153. *Freiheit*, 67, 25 (*LW*, 31:363).
154. Ibid.
155. *De servo arbitrio*. *1525*, WA 18, 754, 1-3: "homo antequam creatur, ut sit homo, nihil facit aut conatur, quo fiat creatura, Deinde factus et creatus nihil facit aut conatur, quo perseveret creatura" (*The Bondage of the Will*, *LW*, 33:342).
156. *Freiheit*, 69, 26 (*LW*, 31:364).
157. *Freiheit*, 68, 26: "Non enim homo sibi vivit soli in corpore isto mortali ad operandum in eo, sed et omnibus hominibus in terra, immo solum aliis vivit et non sibi. . . . Ecce haec est vere Christiana vita, hic vere fides efficax est per dilectionem, hoc est, cum gaudio et dilectione prodit in opus servitutis liberrimae, qua alteri gratis et sponte servit" (*LW*, 31:364-365).
158. *Freiheit*, 73, 27 (*LW*, 31:367).
159. *Freiheit*, 72, 27: "Invicem mutuoque sumus alter alterius Christus facientes proximis, sicut Christus nobis facit" (*LW*, 31:367: "Mutually and by turns we are Christ, the one for the other, doing for the neighbor as Christ did for us").
160. *Freiheit*, 75, 28 (*LW*, 31:369).
161. *Freiheit*, 59, 20 (*LW*, 31:359).
162. We could also say: Between willing and obligation, insofar as it naturally belongs to the essence of the inner man to want to convert his freedom spontaneously and zealously into the deed of love, while the outer man must first be led to it by being mastered by the inner man. The outer man *should* do what the inner man *wills to do*.
163. *Freiheit*, 72, 27: "Vides ergo . . . charitatem, qua liberi, hilares, omnipotentes operatores et omnium tribulationum victores, proximorum servi, nihilominus tamen omnium domini sumus" (*LW*, 31:367).

Notes for pages 84-92

164. *Freiheit*, 59, 20 (*LW*, 31:358).
165. Ibid.
166. *Freiheit*, 59, 20 (*LW*, 31:359).
167. *Freiheit*, 58, 20: "ut cum gaudio et gratis deo serviat in libera charitate" (*LW*, 31:359).
168. *Freiheit*, 66/68, 25: "Non enim alterum tantum sed utrunque verbum dei praedicandum est, nova et vetera proferenda de thesauro, tam vox legis quam verbum gratiae. Vocem legis proferri oportet, ut terreantur et in suorum peccatorum notitiam reducantur, et inde ad poenitentiam et meliorem vitae rationem convertantur. Sed non hic sistendum: hoc enim esset solum vulnerare et non alligare, percutere et non sanare, occidere et non vivificare, deducere ad inferos et non reducere, humiliare et non exaltare. Ideo et verbum gratiae et promissae remissionis ad docendam et erigendam fidem praedicari debet, sine quo lex, contritio, poenitentia et omnia alia frustra fiunt et docentur" (*LW*, 31:364).
169. *Freiheit*, 58/59, 19: "donec in carne vivimus, non nisi incipimus et proficimus, quod in futura vita perficietur" (*LW*, 31:358).
170. *Freiheit*, 78, 29: "ista regula oportet, ut quae ex deo habemus bona fluant ex uno in alium et com[m]unia fiant" (*LW*, 31:371).
171. *Freiheit*, 73, 27 (*LW*, 31:367).
172. *Freiheit*, 72, 27: "Dabo itaque me quendam Christum proximo meo . . . , nihil facturus in hac vita, nisi quod videro proximo meo necessarium, com[m]odum" (*LW*, 31:367).
173. H. Gollwitzer, "Wo kein Dienst ist, da ist Raub," in *Müssen Christen Sozialisten sein? Zwischen Glaube und Politik.* Beiträge von E. Jüngel, H. Gollwitzer u.a., ed. W. Teichert (1976), p. 109.
174. *Freiheit*, 73, 27 (*LW*, 31:367).
175. *Freiheit*, 77/79, 29 (*LW*, 31:371).
176. *Über das 1. Buch Mose. Predigten. 1527*, WA 24, 12, 22-24.

Excursus: The "Inner Man"

1. *The Bondage of the Will, LW*, 33:122; cf. ibid., p. 206.
2. *The Disputation concerning Man, LW*, 34:137.
3. Ibid.
4. Ibid., p. 141.

DATE DUE

HIGHSMITH   #LO-45220